This book is dedicated to Carolyn and to Emily and Samuel, who – despite my passion for natural history – are still my favourite inhabitants of our garden.

a million voices for nature

The RSPB works for a healthy environment rich in birds and wildlife.
It depends on the support and generosity of others to make a difference. It works with bird and habitat conservation organisations in a global partnership called BirdLife International.

If you would like to know more about the RSPB, visit the website at www.rspb.org or write to:
The RSPB, The Lodge, Sandy, Bedfordshire, SG19 2DL; telephone 01767 680551.

Photographers (by page number)

Jani Ahti p36, S.C Bisserot p10, Frank B. Blackburn p26, Joe Blossom p19, Peter Cairns (rspb-images.com) p15, N.A. Callow p31, 89, 103, Laurie Campbell p45, Robert Canis p139, Hugh Clark p104, 138, 143, Andrew Cleave p117, Ron Croucher p55, Stephen Dalton p98, Manfred Danegger p113, Geoff Du Feu p43, 64, John B Free/naturepl.com p155, Chris Gomersall (rspb-images.com) p22, Tony Hamblin (rspb-images.com) p70, Paul Hobson p149, E.A. Janes p127, 152, Rene Krekels/Foto Natura p81, Yves Lanceau p98, 141, Gordon Langsbury (rspb-images.com) p48, Mike Lane (rspb-images.com) p19, Lee Morgan p28, Owen Newman p65, 76, Richard Revels p57, 93, Roy Rimmer p53, Heinz Schrempp p74, Don Smith p27, Paul Sterry p33, 40, 41, 52, 79, 86, 88, 100, 105, 106, 111, 115,119, 125,131, 132, 136, 144, 145,157, Terry Thormin p68, Roger Tidman p12, 17, 19, 140, David Tipling p44, 130, 148, 150, Steve Young p22, 30, 61, 63, 94, Roy Brown, John Ferguson, Michael Lawrence, David Lees (taken from Tracks and Signs) p32

Front cover: Hedgehog Erinaceus europaeus in Flowerpot © Renee Morris/Alamy

First published 2008 by Christopher Helm,
an imprint of A & C Black Publishers Ltd., 38 Soho Square, London W1D 3HB
www.acblack.com

Copyright © 2008 text by Dominic Couzens
Copyright © 2008 illustrations by Peter Partington

The right of Dominic Couzens to be identified as the author of this work has been asserted by him in accordance with the Copyright, Designs and Patents Act 1988

ISBN: 978-0-7136-8534-3

A CIP catalogue record for this book is available from the British Library.

Comissioned by Nigel Redman
Project-managed by Sophie Page and Julie Bailey
Edited by Mike Unwin
Designed by Paula McCann

Proofread and indexed by Janet Dudley

Printed and bound in Singapore by Tien Wah Press (Pte) Ltd

10 9 8 7 6 5 4 3 2 1

SECRET LIVES

OF

GARDEN WILDLIFE

Dominic Couzens
Illustrated by Peter Partington

CHRISTOPHER HELM
LONDON

Contents

Introduction

Of all a garden's many delights perhaps the greatest is intimacy. Whether our patch is a rural expanse, a suburban pocket-handkerchief or a small green corner of a busy street, it is ours. We know it intimately – and better than anyone else does. That is part of its charm.

This intimate retreat is our interface with the outside world. Here, more than anywhere else for most people, we can see the seasons turn. We might visit the countryside to spot catkins at the start of spring or to see the leaves change colour in the autumn, but the garden is the place where we can observe the day-to-day subtleties – and feel them, too. It is here that we can best sense the transformation in the outside world, because we can watch the scene being changed rather than the changing scenes.

But this personal patch of ground, where we plant and prune and feel completely at home, is actually quite an alien world. Down at the base of the grass stems, deep in the leaf litter or high in the tree canopy, life is almost unimaginably different to ours. What must it be like for a butterfly to experience rain or for a wood mouse to walk across frost? We cannot feel these things, and it requires a serious leap of our imagination to get any sense of them.

The animals' world is also a miniature safari park, with all its spectacular conflicts and terrors.

As we stroll across our plush lawns it is hard to imagine the horror a fly must experience in the jaws of a wolf spider, or the frustration felt by a ladybird when rejected by a mate for its only chance in a short breeding season. A shrew tears its prey apart with all the gory violence of a lion, perhaps even more so, and stag beetles lock horns as impressively as rutting deer. These garden dramas may be, if you like, mini-series, but that doesn't make them any less real to their protagonists.

The garden, therefore, is not at all tame. The animals carry on here just as they do everywhere else, without a shred of decorum or the slightest nod to our own sensibilities. Cold-blooded murder, astonishing ingenuity, peculiar sex – it all begins on your doorstep. And in this wild and ruthless place, astonishing stories abound. Some are told here in these pages, many are not. No single volume could contain them all.

We might prefer to believe that our gardens are somehow cleaner and gentler than the rest of the great outdoors. Perhaps that is why we are still so easily surprised when we hear about what goes on within their borders. This book lifts the lid on many truths about our garden wildlife: things that, in our own comfortable world, we might prefer to remain secret.

WHEN THE WINTER garden is covered in frost or snow, it can appear that a dust sheet has been thrown over everything and that all below is silent, still and suspended. But in fact, even throughout the depths of winter, life goes on in the soil, the grass and the leaf litter. Despite appearances, the garden never sleeps.

JANUARY

The Sleeping Garden?

Just hanging around: bats, like these greater horseshoes, are among the garden's few true hibernators.

IT MAY SAY something about the human condition, but a good many of us rather envy the idea of hibernation. The winter, after all, can be trying. We don't like cold and we don't like damp, and the long winter nights can be depressing – even to the detriment of our mental health. Holed up in our centrally heated houses, we all long for the freshness and rebirth of spring, and in such circumstances it can seem a very sensible idea just to sleep the season away.

Perhaps this is why we tend to overestimate the importance of hibernation in the animal life of our gardens. When we look out on a cold, frosty January morning, it is easy to imagine a host of small creatures snuggled away in their winter hideaways, all asleep and snoring, immune to the horrors of the season, and waiting until the days are long and the leaves are out before they awake. But this picture is misleading. The truth is that, in the strictest sense of the term, hardly any garden animals hibernate at all.

Hibernation, in scientific terms, is defined as a long state of torpor, when the body chemistry changes and a sleeping animal is quite immune to the outbreak of a mild, warm spell. In these terms, only bats and hedgehogs fit the hibernation profile correctly. Both are small mammals that, to be active, have to keep their body temperature at around 35°C. In winter,

when food is in short supply, they cannot stoke their inner fires to anything like such levels, so they abandon any notion of doing so and settle down to enter hibernation. Bats head for sheltered places such as holes in walls or trees, or to houses, while hedgehogs tuck themselves away in nests they have built themselves, small constructions of grass or leaves usually wedged under a shrub or bush.

Whilst checked into their hibernation site, these animals experience a profound change in their metabolism. The body temperature of a hedgehog or bat may plunge to 10°C or even lower, and as much as an hour may elapse between short bouts of breathing. The drop in heartbeat rate is even more dramatic: when a small bat is flying, for example, its heart may surge to 1,000 beats a minute, but in deep hibernation this may slow to only 25 beats a minute – just the merest ticking over.

What is important here is that the animals are not just asleep: real chemical changes have occurred in their body. If hibernators are disturbed, they cannot easily be roused as though they had merely been asleep. They linger in their comatose state like human adolescents after a party, and this makes them highly vulnerable to predators. It is therefore important that they choose their hibernation sites very carefully before turning in. The sites must be well hidden as well as sheltered. Bat hibernation sites (known as hibernacula) are often traditional, used each winter by successive generations.

A midwinter wander

Yet among these genuine hibernators, individuals are never inactive for the entire winter season. Both hedgehogs and bats habitually wake up at times for a day or two, stretch their legs or wings, defecate, drink and then resume hibernation – in the bats' case, often at a different location. This is perfectly normal, so should you see either of these animals out and about at this seemingly inappropriate season, you need not worry that they have awoken too early and will succumb to certain starvation. Not at all: if a hedgehog can find some food even as late as Christmas, it can replenish its fat reserves and increase its chances of passing the winter successfully.

Another animal that often wanders around in midwinter is the badger. It cannot truly be described as a hibernator, since its body temperature rarely drops by more than 9°C and often not by much more than 2°C. Nevertheless, January is usually a very quiet time in the sett, with most animals spending much of their time asleep and conserving their energies that way. Scientists, a bit stuck for what to call this state of slumber, tend to refer to it as 'winter lethargy', and badgers can often be seen poking their noses out on warmer January nights.

Many of the animals that you might expect to hibernate properly do not do so at all. You would think that a tiny-bodied mouse or vole would be wise enough to avoid the winter and bed down for the whole season, but the most mice do is to enter into a brief torpor occasionally, with a slight decrease in body temperature. The rest of the time they are active, with small peaks of foraging at dawn and dusk. The secret of survival lies in their winter diet, which consists mainly of autumn fruit and nuts that are present in great abundance in the cold season, while invertebrate food is scarce. Wood mice also live in burrows, which help to insulate them from the cold, and in snowy conditions they can still search around the leaf-litter, or in piles of wood or other neglected parts of the garden, while the snow above further insulates them. They often visit bird tables, too, usually at night when the birds are roosting.

Another group of animals that are widely but erroneously thought of as hibernators are our reptiles and amphibians: namely frogs, toads, newts, lizards and snakes. These animals are cold-blooded and don't regulate their body temperature anyway, so no great internal changes occur in the winter. Instead, they just curl up and remain torpid, while routinely becoming active on warm days. Snakes and toads usually spend the winter in compost heaps or under stones, while frogs – at least, male ones – often settle in the mud at the bottom of a garden pond. They don't drown because they are able to breathe through their skin, and it so happens that the colder water of winter holds more dissolved gases than warmwater. However, ice can be a problem, because this can cause the

Badgers will poke their noses out on mild winter nights.

11

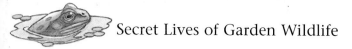
oxygen levels to drop and the amount of dissolved nasties such as carbon dioxide to rise. If the latter reaches a critical level, the torpid frogs will die.

Winter warmers

Of course, no garden creatures are more obvious during the wintertime than birds, none of which even comes close to hibernation. They are active and awake every day, without any significant change in body temperature. Some species, especially those that feed on the summer invertebrate boom, escape winter by migrating to warmer climes, which is a sort of equivalent strategy to hibernation. Swallows, which feed on the same sorts of flying insects as bats, are a good example, flying south about as far as it is possible to go in Africa. But many others remain behind and take their chances with the climate. Most garden birds, such as tits, feed upon berries or nuts, or – like thrushes and blackbirds – guzzle worms and other invertebrates in the soil, which are still reachable except during extreme frosty or snowbound conditions.

Were temperature the only issue, birds would generally have no problems surviving winter weather: their feathers are such good insulators that they effectively go around wrapped in a snug sleeping bag. But birds need fuel, in the form of food, to keep them going, and unless they can find enough, their generators will shut down. In other words, in severe winters birds are more likely to starve than freeze. The great problem of winter is that the amount of darkness greatly exceeds the amount of daylight, so every day is a struggle against time to find enough food to last the night. In December and January, a small bird may spend 90% of daylight engaged purely in the task of foraging. That is why the bird table is usually thronged with customers.

This excess of darkness poses a problem for everyone. But even so, winter can still be a boom time for a few garden residents. No animal thrives in January, for example, quite like the grey squirrel. Individuals of this species often reach their peak weight in January, although they frequently struggle in mid-summer, when other species thrive. The reason for this apparent anomaly, once again, is diet. Squirrels feed

Winter daylight is a precious commodity for a small-bodied bird such as a coal tit.

primarily on nuts, which are a product of autumn. These are stored away in scattered caches, and during winter most squirrels will have plenty in reserve while in summer stocks are at their lowest. The result is summer mortality for squirrels, especially youngsters, but a peak of vigour in winter.

Love in a cold climate

Squirrels' winter vigour translates into what is perhaps the ultimate finger-up gesture to the season: breeding. Providing that the autumn seed crop has been good, the earliest days of the year see a great deal of tree-borne activity among squirrels, making them easily the most conspicuous wild mammals in the garden. And there is a good reason for this friskiness.

Whether or not you like squirrels, their noisy courtship routines are undeniably good entertainment on cold, dreary days. It all begins when a female starts giving off scent to signal her mating intentions. The deliciously feminine fragrance wafts downwind and causes the males, quite literally, to come running. Within minutes a suitor will be hot on the siren's trail and will follow her closely wherever she goes, attempting to attract her attention by the rather unsubtle means of flirting his tail or slapping the tree-trunks with his paws. Soon other males join in and, with her personal space becoming invaded, the female suddenly legs it, dashing away into the trees. The most persistent male immediately follows, and often a marathon chase begins, round and round the tree trunks and up and down branches. It is fast, noisy and teasingly

*Amorous grey squirrels
chase away the winter cold.*

sexy, and you can easily imagine the animals
giggling uncontrollably every time they stop.
At times two or three males may be chasing a
female all at once, and the game may continue
for hours or even days. The garden's treetops
are alive with their noisy, frenetic activity and
general excitement. Eventually the female gives
in and the lucky male mounts her – if he has any
energy left.

Midwinter is also the mating season for foxes.
Foxes are large animals with a wide diet, so they
are well equipped to survive the cold, especially
in gardens where food is readily available. On
winter nights, a fecund male calls loudly to
attract a mate. If he is successful, dog and vixen
will consort and hunt together for a few weeks
until, towards the end of that period, the female
enters oestrus. Fertilisation is only possible for a
mere three days of the year, during which the
pair will copulate frequently. Copulation itself is
protracted, frequently lasting half an hour, but it
has an unexpected peril: if the dog does not
withdraw quickly enough, his penis may become
stuck inside his mate for an hour or more,
making both animals very vulnerable. Coming
across such foxes *in flagrante* is one of winter's
more bizarre sights.

Antifreeze

A surprising number of smaller animals also pass the winter awake and active, in brazen defiance of the conditions. Many of those that live in the soil, such as worms or centipedes, are hardly affected by the winter, although they will burrow deeper if it is extremely cold on the surface. For longer-lived invertebrates, such as black ants, it is business as usual, and even some surface-living creatures, such as wolf spiders, remain active in the grass, seeking out winter gnats and other seasonal morsels.

So, for invertebrates too, our popular definition of hibernation doesn't quite fit, because the cold simply lowers their body temperature without affecting their body chemistry. Some, such as bumblebees, settle into a small hole, where they often lie torpid with their legs in the air, while butterflies such as peacocks and commas settle into tree holes or garden sheds. Many of these hardy invertebrates have glycerol and other compounds in their tissues that effectively act as antifreeze.

The truth is, though, that a great many invertebrates essentially bypass the challenge of surviving winter as an adult by remaining in an immature stage throughout: some as pupae, some as larvae and some as eggs. If the state of hibernation is understood as one in which chemical changes allow the body long periods of inactivity, then perhaps these small creatures are the truest hibernators of all.

Voices of the Night

IT MIGHT SEEM far-fetched to consider a walk in the garden to be an adventure, even if your garden is large, rural and rambling. But what about at night, and particularly in the middle of winter? You may reluctantly have braved the cold to put the bins out or to clear the garden of tools, but have you ever actually lingered outside at such an hour and season? If you did, you might well find it a surprisingly exciting introduction to a completely different world.

There may not be much to look at, especially on a cold night, but the excitement is in the sounds. Even in suburbia the human hubbub eventually dies down by the late evening, whereupon the voices of the night can become clear and true. And January is a surprisingly noisy time: plenty of creatures want to make themselves heard.

The performance, indeed, may start at dusk. Some animals make a song and dance about going to sleep, and you might well hear the loud, pre-roosting clinking calls of blackbirds as the light fades, especially on a gentle evening. Their cries sound like scolding, and sometimes they are: blackbirds often share their roosting bushes, and there can be much bickering about who sleeps where, since some perches – even just centimetres apart – offer better shelter and comfort than others. Scientists also think that some of this commotion may simply be letting off steam, much as young children may reach their noisy zenith at bedtime, only to sink into sleep at the touch of a mattress.

Grey squirrels, too, can be noisy at dusk. Males often spend the twilight chattering and squealing to themselves, for no obvious reason except to fill the air with their soliloquy – they don't hold territories, for instance. Their call is a very distinctive, discordant, strained screech. Sometimes a few more perfunctory chatters precede this squeal, giving the faint impression of a car that is reluctant to start.

Much as the dusk chorus is fun and engaging, however, the real garden safari starts much later at night, when your garden soundtrack can begin to resemble that of a horror movie. This is especially

Every breath you take: a dog fox announces its intentions to any vixen within earshot.

true if you have a local pair of owls, whose calls can turn up the volume on your wandering imagination and send you back inside with heart thumping. The tawny owl is the star here, with its tremulous, far-carrying hoot that broadcasts the terror of the unknown across cities and gardens that seem perfectly tame by day. Most people think that this bird goes '*tu-whit, to-woo*', but that, as written, would be an unusual sequence to hear. Instead the '*tu-woo*' is actually the hoot of the male, a message designed to be heard by other males, while the '*tu-whit*' is a sharp call given by both sexes in conversation. Both sounds are easy to imitate and, indeed, you can fool your listeners into thinking they have heard an out-of-place owl, or even do the same to the bird itself. Indeed, the story is told about two neighbours who went out every night to call out to their local owl and get a response. Only after some years did the neighbours get together one evening for dinner and discover that each man had the same habit of calling to the owl at the same time. Further investigation showed that there was, in fact, no owl in the vicinity: the neighbours had merely been answering each other.

Frosty nights in January, usually deep into the small hours, herald what are perhaps the most atmospheric of all garden sounds: the courtship calls of foxes. The male instigates the conversation, giving a sharp triple-bark that is similar to the bark of a dog, but slightly more questioning in tone. It also has a wilder ring to it: the declaration of an animal without a lead or an owner, up out late and thrillingly free. Meanwhile, the call of the vixen, either made in return or uttered spontaneously, is even wilder and more unsettling. Somewhere between a howl and a scream, it has an air of despair and distress. In reality, of course, the animal feels none of these emotions but, partly because the call is usually heard in the dead of night, it can deeply affect a human listener. There have been

The hooting of the tawny owl is often heard on winter nights.

many occasions when the call of a vixen has been misinterpreted by fretful insomniacs as the terror of a woman, and the police have been called out.

That's part of the night's adventure, of course, not always quite knowing what you are hearing. Late January might also bring the faint purrs and whickering noises of badgers drifting through rural gardens, and a hedgehog might sniff by on its short pause in hibernation. In the countryside an alarmed roe deer may shatter the quiet with its gruff, almost snorting bark. Yet not all the calls can be identified: the fox alone has 28 different vocalisations and the badger 16. And who knows what else might be out there in the darkness?

On certain frosty, starry nights, you might also catch some sounds coming from the sky. They will be sharp, high calls, like a fast intake of breath, punctuating the silence with some regularity. This is the sound of redwings, a species of thrush that filters down in large numbers from northern Europe every winter and wanders nomadically about seeking berries. Redwings move around by night, uttering these sounds to keep their flocks together as they travel the highways of the skies a hundred metres or so above the rooftops. While all the other sounds you might hear on a January night are your neighbours, these calls are made by travellers. To hear them is like hearing the hooting of a distant train: you can only join the journey vicariously, and you wish you could hop on board and see where the dawn finds you. That, certainly, would be an adventure.

Grey squirrels often bed down with their neighbours for the night.

Sleepovers

ANIMALS DON'T PREPARE their winter quarters with half measures: there is no cost-cutting in a squirrel's drey, nor lack of bedding in a mouse's cubbyhole or a badger's sett. Cowboy builders have no place in the animal kingdom, especially since lives are at stake.

At the same time, most animals don't give much quarter to intruders. Small birds tend to roost alone and may react violently when challenged for possession of a good, safe, sheltered site. Mice can wage their small-scale wars, while fighting foxes may leave blood on the ground. For a bird or mammal living out in the wild, a safe sleeping place is as important to their survival as a reliable feeding outlet.

But there are circumstances in which these barriers are broken down – mainly on winter nights. And, surprisingly, the most generous of overnight hosts are grey squirrels. You wouldn't guess this from the way they carry on by day: although squirrels are not territorial, they do observe strict hierarchies and there can be constant bickering between dominant and subordinate animals, with chasing and biting. Tensions may simmer for days between individuals, and the sexual chases of midwinter only serve to stir the competitive juices further, especially between males. You might thus imagine that these would be the very last animals to tolerate sleep-mates in their precious winter nests. Yet oddly, they do.

Grey squirrel sleepovers are so common, indeed, that they can be seen as a survival technique. Even though every individual squirrel will have its own portfolio of winter nests, each will happily slip between the leaves and twigs of

16

another's. It all depends on who is already present inside. A dormitory situation is apparently ideal, and there are records of seven or more individuals crowded inside a single drey – which was presumably built for one. Clearly, the body warmth of bedfellows is enough of an attraction to offset the inconvenience and potential threat of parasites or disease. Interestingly, however, the invitation does not extend just to anyone: the guest must be known to the owner of the drey. Complete strangers are evicted aggressively, yet even love-rivals are tolerated. Males that have been at each other's throats all day in competitive pursuit of the local talent may end up sleeping side by side at night.

Grey squirrels are not the only mammals to extend such an extraordinary invitation. Even badgers, which are usually highly aggressive to any individual outside their social group, will very occasionally tolerate 'guests' in their sett, although these will usually be visitors from a neighbouring territory. They will even share their setts with other species: foxes, rabbits, rats and wood mice may all sometimes become the sitting tenants of badgers.

Birds of a feather

Among birds, there are few more highly-strung characters than the wren. This very small bird has a very big mouth, and its song carries far enough to impart a sort of *Beau Geste* siege mentality around its territory. Wrens don't tolerate other wrens around them. In contrast to many other species of birds, which flock in winter and learn to get along, one wren really is an island. And not surprisingly, wrens roost alone. However, there are occasions when even this anti-social character simply has to relent. These are when conditions outside turn truly life-threatening, when the temperature plunges and every scrap of body warmth simply has to be shared. And thus, on occasion, up to 63 wrens have been discovered crammed into a single nest-box, packed in layers with their heads facing inwards and what tails they have pointing to the outside. These, admittedly, are unusually large aggregations, and small gatherings of half a dozen or so are much more common.

It is not unusual for certain birds to gather together to roost, of course. Starlings are famous for this habit, particularly as they draw attention to themselves before bedding down with remarkable communal aerial manoeuvres, swarming together like bees and sallying back and forth across the sky, all calling in discordant, screeching unison. These roosts, however, and those of blackbirds, gulls and crows, settle down on neutral ground, so there is no host or territory owner who can either drive them off or invite them in. And bird roosts do not, on the whole, consist of birds huddling together to keep warm. Everyone keeps apart at a respectful distance, and a throng of birds in a single spot has a negligible impact on the microclimate.

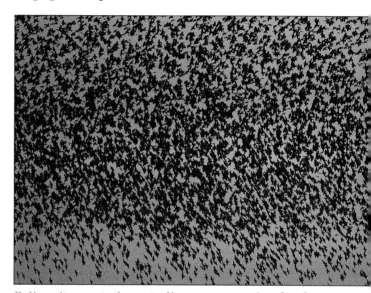

Believe it or not, these starlings are preparing for sleep.

So if birds don't get the benefit of shared body heat in communal roosts, why gather together in the first place? This is a question that has baffled scientists for some time. The obvious increased vigilance of many pairs of eyes is negated by the fact that large aggregations of noisy birds attract predators. So why do they do it? The most recent theories suggest that there might be some useful exchange of information in a roost of birds. If all the blackbirds, finches or starlings in a region come together at night, then any one bird can in theory monitor the state of health of the rest as they arrive: who had a good day's feeding and is feeling bullish, and who didn't. Then, the theory goes, a hungry individual will follow the well-fed individual back to the latter's feeding site in the morning and benefit from a better day.

It's certainly an interesting idea, and could well explain the existence of some bird roosts, but for now the question is still not entirely resolved. And as far as the sleeping squirrel is concerned, none of this matters. All this bedfellow wants is a shared bit of warm fur.

Winter Flora

AS EVERY GARDENER knows, not everything is completely dormant in the midst of winter. As well as some animals being about, there are always some flowers out, too. The first snow-drops creep above the soil, often shooting through the fallen leaves of autumn, breaking the heart of winter and heralding the promise of seasonal change. There can also be early willow catkins; ragged, striking hairdos of yellow witch-hazel; and the blooms of Mahonia and Daphne can turn their own corners yellow or pink respectively. Meanwhile clumps of hellebores and winter-flowering heather whisper their colours softly in the poor light. January colours never shock: they are lush yet subtle, in accordance with the subdued seasonal mood.

The relationship between garden plants and animals is always close, of course. In the summer one cannot miss the humming of insects over flower borders, or the way in which voles, frogs and grasshoppers take to the long grass. In the winter, however, the bond seems to be even more intimate – even though the club contains fewer members. An early bumble-bee is dependent on just a precious handful of types of wintering bloom. And ever-green shrubs and trees, with their leaves intact, stand alone as shelter against the cold and wind.

Few plants are more important for animals at this time of year than ivy. The delights of this creeper are twofold: first, its thick network of waxy leaves attached to a woody stem, usually growing flush against a wall or the trunk of a tree, is about the best possible shelter you can possibly find above ground level in

the garden; second, its first berries appear in January, at a time when the berries of most other trees or shrubs are beginning to run out, so it provides precious food, too.

It is a treat to watch the comings and goings of birds at ivy during a winter's day. At this time of the year, such species of birds as blackbird, song thrush and starling may visit clumps in never-ending shifts, often bickering over stocks like overzealous shoppers at January sales, while ivy is also a favourite of a much less popular bird, the woodpigeon, which gulps it down in enormous quantities. An ivy bush, or indeed any berry-bearing bush that still has some fruit on it, is also likely to attract some more exotic winter visitors, such as redwings or fieldfares from Scandinavia, or blackcaps from Germany, adding a little spice to the garden bird list.

Another berry that is available right now is mistletoe, a parasitic plant that enjoys a working relationship with our largest garden

A mistle thrush guards its precious clump of – appropriately enough – mistletoe.

Left: Pyracantha offers winter berries for blackcaps. Right: Late winter buds make an excellent meal for a bullfinch.

thrush, the mistle thrush. Most birds avoid the white berries, but mistle thrushes often spend hours around a clump that they claim as their own, and will actively defend it from any other birds that come near. In return, when the thrush defecates, the seed is expelled intact, often in the upper branches of a tree, where it can generate. The birds thus act as dispersers for the plant.

Many garden herbivores still dependupon what remains of the autumnal bloom of fruits and nuts. A few, such as jays, nuthatches, mice and squirrels, have stored some of this bounty away in long-term caches, but that does not stop them looking for more on January days or nights. Wood mice, for example, will still be foraging in the garden leaf litter underneath suitable trees for such produce as ash keys, hazel nuts or acorns. Just a single find makes a big difference to a rodent – sometimes life or death.

January's flowers may be sparse in number, but over the last few years their importance has begun to increase as we have experienced warmer winter weather. These days there are regular reports, for example, of colonies of bumblebees remaining open for business throughout the year. Such animals require considerable ongoing sustenance. Warmer weather also rouses such butterflies as brimstones and peacocks from their winter torpor, and they need an urgent source of nectar or pollen to keep them going. Flowers are some-thing of an unusual food source for the garden's larger animals, but both wood mice and house sparrows do have a habit of nibbling bulb plants such as crocuses. Buds, however, are a favourite food of the glorious bullfinch, one of the few birds in the garden to eat soft plant material other than berries, and squirrels take a wide variety of plant

A single nut is a major nutritional find for a wood mouse.

produce in the winter months, including buds, bark and catkins.

Besides ivy, a good many other climbers and shrubs also provide shelter during the coldest months of the year. Although much maligned, *Leylandii* cypress proves to be rather good for roosting birds, while holly also performs this function and has the added benefit of keeping out predators, such as cats, with its prickles. The site and density of the shrub is as important as the species, though. Few real tangles of vegetation will fail to harbour small rodents, birds and a range of invertebrates, including overwintering ladybirds, spiders and ants.

Some of the more intimate relationships between invertebrates and plants play out under the winter microscope. On trees, bark is rarely covered with frost or snow, and its benign micro-climate makes it ideal for any small creature that can crawl inside its nooks and crannies, or bore into it. Stems of many plants, too, provide just enough refuge for the smallest of animals, while others in search of winter shelter simply creep into the cubbyhole of a curled up leaf and hide away as long as the temperature stays low. These animals sometimes depend on just one type of plant, so their dependency on the winter flora is as complete as the early bee searching for a life-saving bloom.

FEBRUARY

WINTER MAY PRESENT

its most brazen face in February, with
bitter winds and thick frosts, but its
influence is inexorably on the wane.
Though birds might still struggle for
survival as they are battered by the
cold, the volume of song increases day
by day. A sharp morning frost may
cover a bed of crocuses, but by the
afternoon their subtle blooms are open
for business from bees. And the ice on
the pond may look thick and impene-
trable on chilly days, but that does not
prevent early frogs and newts slipping
into their breeding waters in between
cold snaps.

A Home of One's Own

Robins sing throughout the winter.

THE DEATH-KNELL of the winter season is a gentle and melodic sound, a destroyer in whispers. February might throw storms and frosts the way of your garden in an attempt to assert itself, but the moment the wind drops and the temperature rises, birds will inevitably sing. They are programmed that way; their inner bodies don't look at meteorological vagaries, but work to a timetable guided by day length. The increasing amount of daylight, albeit murky and grudging daylight, compels them to begin this preliminary stage in their breeding cycle.

By the end of the month, indeed, your garden might be staging quite a concert. Quite simply, every bird species that can sing does so before the end of the month. Robins will cast their shrill, varied questions of complicated prose, punctuated by the loud, repetitive certainty of the song thrush high above in the treetops. Great tits will utter their confident,

The great tit might sound cheerful, but its song is a territorial challenge to others.

cheery two-note chimes, while wrens will shout their over-long phrases from low down in the shrubs. And even the laggards of the season, the chaffinch and blackbird, finally start getting going: the chaffinch offers a simple, accelerating phrase that ends with a flourish, while the blackbird performs fluty mastery. This dark-plumaged virtuoso on the roof may be the last garden bird to start singing in spring, but that is like the star of the show arriving at the climax of the concert. Its varied phrases soothe the ears, gently stealing your attention until you are captivated.

Yet these birds are singing for a purpose, and it is certainly not to charm human listeners: all these songs are claims on your soil. A singing bird has no interest in celebrating the spring or expressing joy; instead it has an urgent need to secure a patch of ground where it can later breed – a territory. It protects its borders by singing in public, so that all around know that its patch is occupied and that there are no vacancies. The song also carries a threat: a singing bird will not voluntarily relinquish the ground upon which it has staked its claim, and will fight, if need be, to keep it.

These are serious messages, and somehow they seems at odds with the euphonious, almost wistful quality that we attribute to much bird song. But so indeed does the identity of the singers. They will almost invariably be males. In bird society it is the preserve of the male to be territorial and to protect the sacred ground where the nest will be built. Females, for their part, keep their mouths shut during this season and await the outcome of the vocal bouts. On the whole, they will, upon pairing,

move into a territory that has already been defined and defended for them.

This business of territory is exceedingly important for a bird. Usually a male will fail to breed, and even to survive unless he manages to acquire one and keep it. His plight, though, is a common one. Many other garden animals face the same predicament and have the same need for a place of their own where they can bring up broods without constant harassment. To understand this, imagine a garden as a hotel: it has a limited number of rooms suitable for each client, and somehow or other, they must all be booked up for the coming season.

Family rooms

There are several interesting differences between garden birds and garden mammals when it comes to territory. Pursuing the hotel analogy, birds tend to check in as singles, with a double bed made up for the potential mate to come later; mammals, on the other hand, tend to book up family suites, to cater for group living.

Take foxes. Although it is unusual to see more than one at a time, and many people consider them to be solitary animals, they don't actually live alone. It is perfectly possible to find a territory occupied by just a dog and a vixen, but usually there are more individuals sharing a territory, and sometimes these social groups can grow to quite a crowd: remarkably, there can be as many as ten adults sharing the same area. On the whole, these individuals tend to be blood relatives so, for example, the dog and vixen may share their territory with one or two cubs from previous years. But this is not always the case: in the winter, especially, young dog foxes that have dispersed from elsewhere may successfully

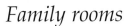

Battle by the bins: two rival foxes meet.

accede to membership. They come in search of females on heat, and sometimes these Johnny-come-lately males are able to pair up successfully with one of the vixens in the group.

Although foxes can be noisy, they tend not to defend their territories by voice, as birds do. Instead, and overwhelmingly, they use scent. As just about anyone who spends much time outside could tell you, foxes have a pungent smell – even to us. Their urine carries a lot of information, and foxes may sometimes pee more then a hundred times a night – although never more than a few drops at a time. When out on patrol they routinely leave marks on anything they find that is new, and over time the whole territory – and especially its border areas – becomes suffused with the scent of the resident social group. It is thus all too easy for an intruder to know when it is trespassing, and for the incumbent animals to recognise any visitor as a stranger.

The difference in greeting gestures between those performed when the paths of two members of a social group cross, and those when two strangers have an encounter, is so different as to almost be comical. When group members meet they act like two 'luvvies' at a party, with effusive wags of the tail and meaningful nuzzling. If two strangers meet, however, there will be snarling, threatening and aggressive arching of the back – in fact, just like two luvvies at a party when only one of them is employed.

Badgers have similar domestic arrangements to foxes. They, too, hold group territories, often with five or more adults in residence, and once again there may be close family ties within the group. Another feature shared with their fellow carnivores is that a strict hierarchy is maintained to keep order, with the dominant boar holding a somewhat autocratic sway over everybody else. He ensures, by barging everyone around, that his smell attaches to all his minions and acts as a communal badge. The dominant sow also tends to be overbearing and bullying, and often bites the subordinate members of the group to keep them in their place.

Sett and match

February is a very exciting month to be watching badgers, because of a weird quirk of timetabling in their lives. This is the month when the cubs are born, but it is also the height of the next courtship season, when there is much hanky-panky around the sett and all the animals are extremely excited. What happens is that the sows, once they have given birth, become extremely receptive to the male again after the sleepy lull of winter's depth. The eggs in their ovaries can once again be fertilised, a phenomenon known grandly as post-parturient oestrus, and copulation is common, despite the patter of tiny feet around the sett. In fact, badgers have been recorded copulating in every month of the year and yet, without fail, they invariably deliver their one brood in the late winter. How can this be? The answer is that, even though the eggs of the female badger might have been fertilised early in the year, they are not implanted until the autumn, and only then if the sow is in the right condition. Therefore, once the babies have been born, they are all ready and raring to go.

February fever: it's the courtship season for badgers.

The general receptiveness of a badger sow from February onwards is a trigger for many of the young males in badger society to strike out and improve their lot in life. They all, remember, began life in social groups under the iron grip of a dominant boar and there comes a time when this begins to grate. Thus, many males leave their home sett and wander around in search of a new life and, in particular, a lusciously fertile sow. Not surprisingly, these youngsters meet opposition to their plans, but all over the country in February the rank of dominant boar in a sett can fall to one of these upstart usurpers. These conflicts, combined with the purring and whickering of a randy suitor as he fusses over his mate, and the general excitement of having cubs below, makes the February badger soap opera riveting for those prepared to sit out the cold and watch it.

Badgers and squirrels might share the same garden, but that, it seems, is pretty much all they have in common – at least as regards their territorial behaviour and domestic arrangements. For a start, the squirrels don't live in groups, or even as a pair, but independently. The females look after the young all by themselves. Neither do squirrels defend territorial borders. But every animal will certainly have its own sphere of operation: a home range, a place where it knows the layout of the trees and can hide away its winter store of nuts. So, while squirrels leave scent marks of urine to let the community know that they are around, they do not defend anything as their own. They are more interested in their position in the local hierarchy, which ultimately determines how much access they will have to all the resources they need.

Life in the colonies

It would be apt to describe the arrangements in squirrel society as moderately informal, but compared to bats they are positively totalitarian. Bats should be hibernating in February – although on mild nights you might spot one out and about – but the fact is that, even as they hang torpid, these small mammals are still highly sociable. Bats are almost never alone. They hibernate together, roost together, breed together and leave their roosts for hunting trips at about the same time. Only when they are feeding might you see just one or two, but even then they will invariably bump into other bats doing the same thing, just as we might bump into other people when out shopping.

However, bat relationships seem to lack depth. Although their gatherings are often termed 'colonies', there seems to be little co-ordination and virtually no long-term interaction between their members. In fact, bats routinely move between colonies, so that they can be roosting in one site on one night and at another the following night, and there is scant evidence of hierarchies. Bats would seem to have very open societies, in which everyone is entitled to be a member of almost any group. The only exception is summertime roosts, which are open only to young mothers and immature bats of either sex.

Down in the leaf litter or long grass, the small terrestrial mammals of our gardens give an informative, if complicated lesson on how and why differing domestic arrangements might work themselves out. In the females, territoriality is related to food supply. In species whose food is readily available in vast quantities, such as short-tailed voles, which eat mainly grass, there isn't much point in defending a territory because resources are not limited. The females thus come and go as they see fit. In species with more choosy diets, however, such as wood mice, which eat seeds that are available only from certain plants, it pays to defend your resources from others. So the female wood mice mark their territory, encircling stands of herbs or patches of ground below nut-bearing trees.

Male rodents, by contrast with females, work out their territories around the availability of females. They have to eat, of course, and are perfectly capable of defending resources, but what determines their actual range is the availability of mates. Here the arrangements of the male short-tailed vole and wood mouse differ. The former compete amongst themselves for a patch of ground, which they defend; once installed, they will have access to any non-territorial females that visit, thus maximising their mating possibilities. The latter, on the other hand, would limit their access to females by maintaining a territory, so instead they wander widely, visiting the maximum number of female territories – although their home range, the sphere of operation, may be shared with other males.

If these rodent arrangements tell us anything, it is that the social lives of our garden animals and birds are complicated and finely tuned. As each February night draws in, the garden hotel is fully booked, with just about every kind of room on offer taken.

A light-lightweight contest between two wood mice.

Extrasensory perception

THE GARDEN IS such a familiar place, and its animals such everyday neighbours, that it can be easy at times to forget how very different to us the wildlife on our patch can be. We might expect animals to breathe, work and put their feet up just as we do, but in reality their lives are utterly and completely alien. They all, for example, partake in an everyday struggle to survive, the likes of which we in the modern western world have long forgotten. Many are nocturnal and are uncomfortable in the light of day. And nowhere is the gulf between human and animal more obvious than in the way we respectively perceive our surroundings.

A good example of this gap in perception concerns a creature that often shares our living quarters: the house mouse. It is fair to say that, unlike humans, its main method of communication is by scent rather than sight, and any territory is marked out, not by 'no trespassing' notices, but by trails of urine. A male house mouse patrolling its territory drops urine at a rate of no less than 100–200 depositions per hour, while females are rather less porous, peeing a mere 25–100 times an hour. Sometimes, if they are feeling especially exclamatory, they leave droppings as well. Unfortunately for our hygiene concerns, mice will leave their body

With their battery of efficient non-visual senses, mice, like this house mouse, are quite comfortable in the dark.

The dead of night: barn owls can catch rodents in complete darkness.

fluids on everything they touch, and they will thus often recognise novel objects in their territory by virtue of these being scent-free. This universality of scent marking is very helpful to mice, because urine contains a great deal of information: the sex, species and reproductive status of the individual that is in residence, plus perhaps even details of its social position and state of health.

Mice also communicate by sound, and sometimes we can hear them squeak. Apparently the sounds that they make are only audible in our register on certain occasions, usually when the rodents are fighting or being severely threatened, but female house mice, wood mice and bank voles will also protest audibly when rejecting the advances of males – so at least there is some common ground between rodent and human! For much of the time, however, small mammals actually make ultrasonic clicks, which are too high pitched to be audible to the human ear. Babies do this when in distress and, conversely, males make triumphant ultrasonic bursts when approaching, winning over and mounting females. Meanwhile, house mice have poor vision, although they can pick up movement and some rough detail. What with this, their ultrasonic clicks and astonishingly

sensitive noses, house mice really are little aliens.

Of course rodents are not the only mammals that can detect and use ultrasound. Bats rely on it and, let's face it, these aerial mammals really are other-worldly – easily trumping many science-fiction movie monsters in their bizarre appearance. They squeak out ultrasonic pulses and listen for the echoes coming back in order to catch their food, which they can do in complete darkness. This technique is known as 'echolocation' and is similar in principle to how dolphins catch fish under water.

The obvious conclusion about bats is that they have no need to see light and therefore must be blind. This is actually false, so if you are ever officiating a sports competition and an angry competitor accuses you of being 'as blind as a bat', you should take comfort from the reality. Tell your accuser that, in common with a bat, you do see best in low light levels but are perfectly capable otherwise. Bats don't see in colour, but they can use their eyes to find their way around using landmarks, and some, such as the long-eared bat, are also thought to use their eyes to help catch food.

Several of our most familiar garden creatures have other quirks of vision. Foxes and hedgehogs, for example, don't see colour very well at all, while squirrels, despite being diurnal, see most things in shades of grey – except for yellow, which they see perfectly well. Each of these animals is particularly sensitive to movement, which means that, if you stay still, they will often approach you closer than you might expect.

Birds, meanwhile, have quite similar visual perception to humans. Even owls, which are famed for their extraordinary eyesight in the dark, in fact don't see very much better in poor light than we do – although, in common with a number of nocturnal hunters, they do pick up movements rather better than us. (In fact, in darkness, owls are outperformed by frogs and toads.) Most birds see the full range of colours that we do – which explains why, in contrast to furry mammals, birds are usually much more colourful themselves.

Birds do outscore us in one visual way, though: they can – or at least some of them can – perceive ultraviolet light. This must help in the autumn, for example, when they are searching for berries. Many berries are blue in colour and have an ultraviolet component, which must make them stand out very brightly against the green or brown of an autumn bush.

In recent years it has been shown that the ultraviolet side of life can be important to one of our most familiar birds, the humble blue tit. However much we watch the comings and goings of the bird table, it can be very difficult indeed to tell individuals apart, unless one or more is particularly scruffy or has lost feathers somewhere. But the blue tits themselves can certainly tell each other apart, because the degree of ultraviolet reflectance from their bright cap, on top of their head, varies. Some birds have brighter caps than others and it is these individuals that do better than their rivals in the reproductive stakes. Among blue tits, ultraviolet reflectance is sexy.

Another way in which animal perceptions can differ from our own is in their dimensional aspect, and nothing illustrates this better than the

hearing of the barn owl, which sometimes visits more rural gardens. Most garden animals are quite good at perceiving the direction of a sound, usually by sensing the time lag between the arrival of the signal in one ear relative to another. For example, if a sound comes to us from the right, it reaches our right ear before the left ear and the difference computes its direction. But for most animals, this information is limited in its efficiency to two dimensions. In the nocturnal barn owl, however, it so happens that one ear is placed higher in the skull than the other. This exaggerates the time lag heard by the respective ears in the vertical as well as the horizontal plane, so the barn owl has some astonishing capabilities. It can catch a mouse in complete darkness, homing in on its victim with a margin for error of a mere one degree.

Looking like an other-worldly alien in your garden, the long-eared bat's face reflects its amazing sensory adaptations.

A worm-hunting badger indulges its greatest passion.

Only here for the worms

MUCH AS YOU might be proud of your garden and the way in which your hard labour has made it a haven for wildlife, I'm afraid that I have a sobering fact for you. A good many of your visitors aren't bothered by what you have done: they are only after your worms. You can therefore feel a little like the chef who specialises in fish, yet night after night the customers order only burgers.

Worms really are the bog standard of garden food, with a list of customers that would make most fast food joints blush. Mind you, worms are not your typical fast food: not only can they be thoroughly awkward to catch, and therefore hardly quick and easy, but their nutritional value is incontestable. Once unearthed, however, they are pleasingly easy to handle: not too big, not too small and no biting teeth. They are packed with bundles of muscle (required to help them burrow), a little roughage and just enough

fluid to satisfy your thirst. If your mouth is watering reading this, don't be surprised: human beings have regularly eaten earthworms without any ill effects.

It is quite astonishing, too, how many garden animals eat them. And even more so, how many actually depend on worms. Take the badger, for instance. That heavily built, sharp-toothed predator, with its tremendously powerful front paws, turns out to be largely the finished product of an awful lot of worm eating. In some of its worldwide range the badger has a catholic diet, with beetles and other insects predominating, and it is more than capable of despatching rabbits and other larger animals, but here in western Europe earthworms comprise about half the badger's entire annual diet. On a good mild, damp night when conditions are ideal, one individual will eat about 200 worms, and during the course of a year it can rack up about 20,000.

29

Another fearsome predator is the hedgehog. Although in the 'wild' hedgehogs benefit from a broad diet, in gardens it seems that they feed mainly on worms, unless they receive takeaways from householders. One of the reasons for this is lawns. These miniature manicured grasslands are ideal for a small mammal that keeps its nose permanently close to the ground, while on the other hand they offer little sanctuary to worms if the grass is kept short and neat. The trouble for worms is that they have to come out of their holes in order to mate, and when hedgehogs are on the prowl that can be a costly mistake.

At least the worms only have to contend with hedgehogs during the spring and summer, when the latter are awake, and so can relax a little when the spiny predators are hibernating. This isn't the case with shrews. These small, voracious mammals are relentless worm guzzlers at any time of year and, worse still, they are active night and day, taking only small breaks, like miniature carnivorous company executives. The only saving grace is that a single large worm makes a pretty good meal for a shrew, so the carnage perpetrated by badgers never reaches the same gruesome levels. Just a handful of worms every 24 hours keeps a garden shrew full up.

You might think that the worms could avoid such losses by keeping their heads down and staying in the soil. But that doesn't work in some gardens because of another year-round worm predator the mole. Moles, of course, live underground in a network of tunnels and inevitably, on occasion, worms must cross these burrows – just as it is impossible for us to walk far without crossing a road. As moles patrol their walkways there is therefore almost always a juicy worm waiting for them somewhere in the network. Moles can consume up to 25 earthworms in the course of a night's work. If they catch more than this they will readily cache the excess. Naturally, they cannot put them behind bars, but instead they bite the worm's end off, which immobilises it until they return.

Birds, of course, are also famous for their knack of catching worms. And it's not just the early birds that are successful, but any hunter who has acquired the considerable skills involved. Diurnal, surface-dwelling wormers must detect quite subtle visual cues, such as a worm's posterior sticking out when making a cast. If you watch a blackbird or a song thrush on a lawn, you will see that it also uses its ears. A bird will often simply stand still on the lawn, with its head cocked to one side, carefully picking up the sound of wiggling near the surface. Then, suddenly, it will pounce and pull the worm out with what it hopes is a single tug. This is one of those few times when you can witness a worm fighting back. Worms are very muscular, and their chaetae, the tiny 'legs' that

A mistle thrush tugs hard, but the worm won't give up without a fight.

help them move through the soil, are backward pointing, so it can require a very considerable effort to drag a reluctant worm into the light.

Apart from blackbirds and thrushes, a good many other garden birds also eat worms. Robins take plenty, and even tawny owls will often visit your lawn on a damp night to pounce on mating 'pairs'. And I haven't yet mentioned the foxes, frogs, toads and newts. Even some snails eat worms, catching them after what must be one of the slowest chases in the animal kingdom.

Somehow, though, despite this slaughter, worms continue to inhabit our gardens, recycling our leaves and aerating the soil. Their key to survival is their extraordinary abundance. Counts vary, but the average garden will probably host 10,000–100,000 worms, virtually all of them living in the top 25cm of the soil.

Remarkably, some worms have been known to live for ten years or more, and they don't become reproductively active until they are two

Feeling hungry?

years old. These figures suggest that, despite the enormous toll taken on them as a whole, worms are better survivors than we might imagine. And that's just as well. For without these remarkable creatures, the garden would be a drab and lifeless place indeed – just like a restaurant without customers.

Nature detective

THERE IS SOMETHING about the wildness of any garden that is alluring and exciting. The patch of ground you call your own may not be very remote, especially if it is on top of a tower block or set among the suburbs, but that doesn't stop it being wild. The fact is, your birds, insects and frogs are not domestic. You only have so much influence over your animal visitors and, in the end, you are in thrall to them. Garden wild animals are free to go where they wish, and, despite their proximity, their lives and decisions are quite remote from ours.

One of the ways in which this is most apparent is in most animals' tendency to avoid us. We might know we have foxes in the garden by hearing them at night, but any meetings we have tend to be fleeting and chance. The same applies to many others, such as wood mice or shrews. Sometimes we might suspect these elusive animals are there, but have no proof. We never see them at all.

However, there are ways in which we can compensate for the elusiveness of wildlife and at the same time satisfy an urge in ourselves. We can don our detective's coats, turn up all

our senses to full and become a tracker. It is surprisingly easy to do and often remarkably revealing. Even on the coldest of February mornings you can still read the events of the night before, even if it's only from the boldest signs that even an apprentice could decipher.

Of course, if it has snowed, we might well find animal tracks laid out before us. But realistically, unless the snow is crisp and hard, all we can identify is that an animal has passed, and that it is of a particular size. We have a better chance if it has rained overnight and there are tracks in the mud. But we will never see many. Bird tracks are easy to recognise because they show four toes facing forward and the other back. Crows quite commonly leave such tracks as they meander over the lawn. As for other tracks, these tend to be easier to recognise than to find: fox tracks are a little like those of a dog, but narrower, with all the toe pads of similar size; squirrel tracks have distinctive long soles, and delicate toes and fingers; and deer hooves leave an unmistakable double indentation.

One track that does not quite fit into this category, but is a track nonetheless and a good indicator of nocturnal perambulations, is the shiny trail of a snail. These little ribbons of slime can often remain after a still, dry night, and should not be discounted. The suspects can easily be followed.

But tracks are a rarity. Let's get down to the real business: quite frankly, if you wish to be a nature detective, you must be prepared to get stuck into droppings. And here, the easiest animal to detect is the fox. When foxes move about they urinate constantly and, if they discover something prominent or of particular interest, they defecate on it. Thus, if you find somewhat slug-shaped droppings on a stone, on a mound, or even on some food that you have put out, that is the work, so to speak, of a fox. These droppings will also smell unmistakably of the animal and indeed the musty scent may hang in the air long after the sprayer has gone to ground.

Droppings are certainly informative, and various books will regale you with details and diagrams. Squirrel droppings look a bit like those of rabbits, but are a little smaller, while those of mice and voles might well be familiar to you if you keep hamsters or gerbils. Meanwhile, if you are a dweller in the heart of a city, you might have to content yourself with identifying bird droppings instead. Yes, you have to admit it: pigeon droppings may not be pleasant, but they are at least a sign.

Of course one dropping that is easily seen is the cast of a worm. These small spirals of egested earth are not made by our common earthworm, *Lumbricus terrestris*, but by some relatives called *Allolobophora*. Wet winter nights are best.

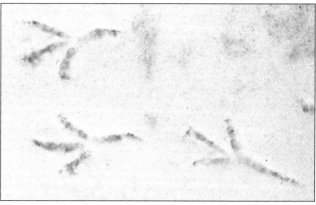

Above: This is what real crow's feet look like.

Left: The 'Abominable' fox has passed this way.

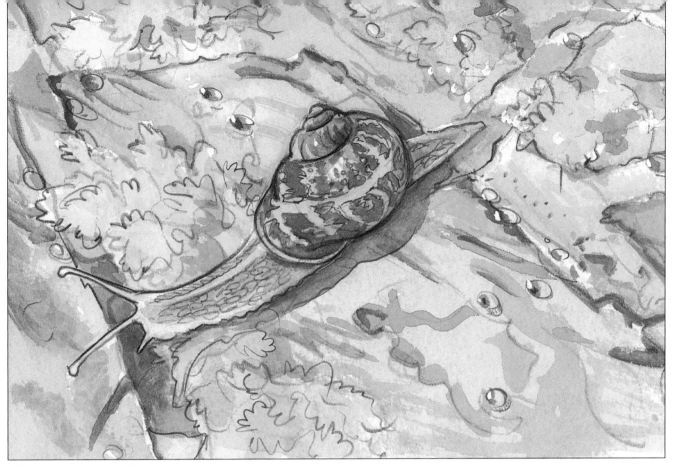

Slime dancing: a snail leaves its trail.

Droppings are not the only sign of feeding. Herbivorous animals may well leave damaged cones and nuts in their wake, and these are often possible to trace. For example, if you have coniferous trees in your garden or local area, it is easy to tell how some of the fallen cones have been dealt with. Squirrels gnaw them with frightening precision and intensity, leaving the centre of the cone with all the scales gnawed – a little like how we leave corn-on-the-cob. Mice don't perform quite such a hatchet job, just gnawing one side of the cone, or chewing off a few of the scales. Woodpeckers, when they work cones, leave a scene of deformity and devastation.

Different animals also handle nuts differently. Squirrels often split them in two equal halves, if they are small enough, while birds such as great tits merely

Cones chewed by squirrels have all the scales neatly severed.

peck a hole in them. Small mammals such as mice chew a round hole in one side of the nut, just big enough to squeeze the kernel out. Some animals, annoyingly, even bury nuts in the lawn. If you find signs of excavation, the suspects include squirrels, foxes, magpies, carrion crows and jays. Green woodpeckers also make holes in order to reach ant nests, even in February, but their holes are usually smaller and more precise. These birds use regular work-benches, known as anvils, where the cones are lodged into pieces of hard wood and hacked apart.

Finally, you might be unlucky enough to find a corpse in your garden, and on such occasions you can often identify how the victim has died. Most mammal corpses will probably be those from fox kills. If the corpse is a bird, look to see whether any feathers are broken: if they are, the culprit is probably a fox again, as this animal bites through feathers; if not, the killer is probably a sparrowhawk, which plucks feathers from the corpse with precision. Visible sparrowhawk kills are often just a mass of white feathers, usually those of pigeons. Sometimes more of the corpse remains, but with the head removed.

As you examine the corpse and consider the kill, it should not be lost on you that you have become the garden's forensic examiner. The garden has a body, and with it a mystery. Enter you, the householder and private detective.

IT MAY HAVE looked in February as though little was changing outside as the winter tried to cling on. But by March a completely different mood has settled over the garden. The crocuses and snowdrops are already past their peak, while daffodils sit around in bunches around the place like picnickers at a garden party. From nest-building birds to foraging bumblebees, and from spawning frogs to suckling squirrels, there is suddenly an air of visibility and activity. The spring is beginning to take off, and nobody wants to be left behind.

MARCH

Settling In

Opening time: an early bumblebee tucks into a crocus.

BIG SIGNS AREN'T always the most instructive signs, and in the spring garden, much as the daffodils, forsythia and grape-hyacinth blooms shout out their seasonal message like advertising hoardings, the smaller changes around them are more significant. After all, these showy flowers are but transient, whereas bumblebees, for example, working at their blooms or hugging the ground, will be around for the whole summer, and their quiet, unfussy progress allows us a much deeper insight into the changing season. For these lovable, furry workaholics, March is a time of intense preparation. In common with many garden animals, they have much groundwork to do.

Bumblebees spend the winter in a torpid state, often dozing away in a small hole in the ground. They are, however, among the earliest of all insects to emerge in any numbers, and it only takes a slight amelioration in the weather to get their engines going and tempt them out into the weak sunshine. Once awake, huge tasks lie ahead for them: each has a responsibility, no less, to found an entire colony.

The bumblebees that awaken in spring all fit the same profile: autumn and winter have taken their toll on the workers and males, and the only remaining survivors are queens. It is their duty to perpetuate the species. They have already mated and so carry the raw materials to create a colony, but that will come later. First they must look after themselves. They visit spring blooms in search of both pollen and nectar, and feed intensively to replenish the fat reserves they lost during the winter. Their strength builds up little by little, and by about the end of the month they have enough energy to begin their second important task: house-hunting. Bumblebees nest in warm, sheltered places, and when you see one in spring flying especially low to the ground, or even walking upon it, you can be sure that it is searching out likely holes. However, finding a suitable site, with the necessary floral resources nearby to support a whole colony of 40 or more adults nurturing new queens, is not always easy. Many fail.

Those that succeed then perform the apian equivalent of putting their feet up and making themselves a cup of tea. They fashion a tiny cup from wax, and in it place regurgitated nectar. This is a 'honey pot', from which they can sup during difficult weather to keep themselves going and, eventually, begin the process of nurturing their first eggs.

Bumblebees are not the only garden creatures that awaken during March. The garden's hibernating mammals may also do so, although bats will not become truly active until some time in April or even May, and will sink back to sleep after a short sojourn, while only the earliest hedgehogs awaken enough to get dressed for work, so to speak. For both these animals any period of waking is used to find food; their fat reserves can become perilously low at such a time. For the bats, this means trying to locate the meagre supplies of flying insects that come out on early spring nights, while hedgehogs will be searching primarily for earthworms and larger insects – unless, of course, they manage to cadge titbits from admiring householders.

The garden's amphibians are far less sleepy by March because – unlike, for example, bats – they are on a tight schedule. They need to get breeding underway to ensure that metamorphosis proceeds to the non-aquatic stage before tadpoles are left trapped in shrinking pools by the heat of summer. Most of our amphibians have lasted the winter under rocks or in other sheltered nooks and crannies. In early spring they join a wholesale movement towards their breeding ponds.

It's not quite rush-hour, but toads are on the move.

March of the migrants

Such movements of amphibians are, effectively, migrations. They may not cover the immense distances recorded for birds or insects, but they do involve large numbers of animals travelling to a certain place with a definite purpose, which is the essence of migration. Frogs, toads and newts tend to make a bee-line for the pond in which they were born, and recent studies of frogs has suggested that they probably use their sense of smell to find their way 'home'. This attachment to the natal pond is quite strong: both frogs and toads have been seen swimming across what look like perfectly suitable breeding ponds on their way to the correct address. Toads are especially resolute in their determination to reach the 'right' pond. Frogs less so. One suspects that, were both species subjected to interrogation, the frogs would be the first to crack.

These spring amphibian migrations can be an impressive spectacle, although they tend to happen on warm, damp nights when gardeners have downed tools for the day. Toads, in particular, have a habit of migrating in large numbers, as though they all travelled on a bank holiday, and you may sometimes be fortunate enough to see dozens crossing your lawn or driveway all at once. They are quite comically single-minded about something for which, let's face it, they are not very well designed: long-distance walking. Dragging themselves over walls, and through fences and long grass, they resemble those charity marathon runners encumbered with ludicrous fancy dress for their twenty-six miles. Toads don't walk that far, usually not much more than a mile, but this – in relative terms – is a Herculean effort. Every garden watcher should try at least once to line the route of a toad migration: it can be one of the real spectacles of spring.

March also sees the first arrivals of more familiar migrants, birds such as swallows and chiffchaffs. Although the former and some of the latter will be coming in from Africa, they tend to look a lot leaner and fitter than the earthbound frogs and toads, avoiding that Heathrow-arrivals hall-look, and sometimes sing merrily within moments of settling in.

By contrast with most small birds, male and female long-tailed tits share in nest construction.

Builders

Incoming migrant birds have some catching up to do. By March, virtually all the garden's resident species, such as blackbirds and robins, have set up their territories and obtained a mate, a process that has not yet started for the new arrivals. Remarkably, however, a swallow can still fit two broods into a season lasting from April to August, which is as many as most resident species can manage, even with their head start. The migrants just sort out their preliminaries more quickly and get on with the job.

March is a good time to see birds building nests. Some species begin well before the trees acquire their leaves, giving garden watchers time to appreciate the intricacies of the process. Woodpigeons and collared doves fly about with telltale sticks in their bills, and wrens carry small pieces of dried grass or leaves. Despite their best efforts at secrecy, you can often find their structures quite easily; a quick peek is enough, however, and it is actually illegal to disturb them. In the garden, no bird makes more fuss about its efforts than the long-tailed tit, which can take a laborious three weeks to complete its domed effort. Most of this is expended in acquiring the right materials: moss, bound with strands of spider's webs, constitutes the main structure; lichens are needed for the camouflaged outside and feathers for the well-insulated interior. Each morning you can watch the birds going back and forth to their equivalent of the DIY superstore, exhaustively securing thousands of nuts and bolts in place. At the end of this long process they will have completed a marvellous feat of engineering: warm, well concealed and elastic enough for a growing family. Sadly, a high proportion of nests fail, making them small white elephants in thorny bushes. The problem seems to be inherent in the building process. By making so many trips, and in beginning construction before the leaves can conceal their activities, the long-tailed tits drew unwitting attention to themselves and their nests.

Bringing feathers, to line the comfy interior, marks the last stage in the building cycle.

High-rise and low rent

Up in the trees some nests are stirring with youngsters, even this early in the year. Carrion crows, rooks and mistle thrushes are all early breeders in gardens and suburbs, and their respective nests may host the chipping of eggs by the end of the month. The early start is connected to the availability of earthworms, which are a staple food for the youngsters. If the rooks were to start breeding later, the drier soil of the warmer season could drive the earthworms deeper down than in the moist spring, making it harder to find enough of them.

You wouldn't immediately know it, but March is also peak time for the first births of squirrel youngsters. From the outside the drey is quiet, but you can spot the unmistakable signs of proud parenthood in the behaviour of the incumbent. A nursing female squirrel is highly aggressive to any squirrels who might stray past, causing an intermittent noisy commotion, and she also tends to stick within 100m of her nest for the time her young are there, rather than wander around as squirrels generally do. Having mated in January, the female will have spent considerable time and energy constructing a special litter drey for her nursing period, and this might be slightly bulkier than the other dreys in the vicinity. But really one has little idea of what is going on unless the drey is seriously disturbed or, for some reason, the female becomes unsettled. Then you might be fortunate enough to witness the mother moving her babies, of which there are usually three, from one drey to another, clasping them by the neck gently in her jaws.

Down on the ground, March is also a highly significant month for foxes. They, too, are giving birth. And unlike squirrels, which also have summer litters, this is their one and only time in the year. There are usually about four or five cubs in a fox litter, and a sure sign that they have been born is a visit from the dog fox, carrying an item of food. Just prior to the birth the vixen expelled him from the earth. But now the food he brings is vital, because his young – not yet able to regulate their own body temperature – cannot be left alone. Indeed, it might not just be one dominant dog that pays a visit, but any member of the social group, each bringing its own contribution. It's rather like visiting hours at a maternity ward, except that nobody brings flowers.

Of course, garden foxes are often just that, bringing up their babies right on the householder's property. A particularly popular site for both urban and suburban foxes is under a garden shed, and this retreat may provide home to no less than 40 per cent of all litters. Foxes are also adept at squeezing between small openings (as little as 10cm), and will frequently creep beneath occupied houses to raise their young, exploiting the warmth and space to be found beneath the floorboards. Other sites include woodpiles, derelict buildings and dense vegetation above ground. And, of course, they can always revert to natural type and actually dig an earth – although in gardens this often tends to be under lovingly nurtured flowerbeds and rockeries, much to the outrage (at least initially) of the gardener.

Wherever they are born, fox cubs come into the world naked and with their eyes shut. For two weeks they remain helpless, then both eyes and ears begin to open. Like many other garden animals in March, they awaken to an early spring, with a long summer season of action and learning ahead of them.

Back in the cub-house: a family of foxes under a garden shed.

Frogs Need Hugs

THERE ALWAYS SEEMS to be something a little unwholesome about amphibian reproduction. Whether it's the writhing masses in the pond, the feeble dirty-old-man croaking, or the indecorous state of male and female stuck together in public like two shameless adolescents, the whole performance just seems a little bit crass and undignified.

The reason for this is quite simple, however. Frogs – and toads and newts as well – reproduce externally, which a polite way of saying that the male lacks a penis and therefore cannot get his sperm inside the female's ovary. This state of affairs is responsible for two characteristics of amphibian coupling: the sometimes torrid free-for-all among males crammed into the shallow end of your pond and the unsubtle sight of a male clasped firmly on the back of a female, a position known as amplexus.

The need for amplexus is not difficult to explain. A female frog full of eggs is a bit like a balloon. She devotes the early part of the year to mass production, and as her count of unfertilised eggs increases she begins to get heavier and heavier. By the middle of March she becomes so

grotesquely plump that you feel she could burst at any time – and this is effectively what she does. One March night, usually at about 3.00am, she massages her tummy a little and then, quite suddenly, ejects her entire collection of eggs in one go. Several hundred emerge and eventually stick together in a single gelatinous clump – the characteristic frogspawn known to almost any gardener with a pond.

This sudden and wholesale dumping of eggs creates a very specific problem for the male frog: in order to fertilise them he must be present at the very moment they are laid and alert enough to shed his sperm as they emerge. It would be no good trying to swim over the spawn after it is ejected, since the protective jelly surrounding the eggs quickly swells up and effectively slams the door shut to fertilisation. The donor male must therefore be in exactly the right place at exactly the right time.

And that place, inevitably, is on top of the female. This is the reason for amplexus. The male cannot be certain quite when the female will lay the eggs, so he clasps her around the belly and holds on grimly, ready for action at any time.

Waiting for the moment...

Frog spawn: what all the fuss is about.

Everywhere the female goes, so he goes – by piggy-back. Amplexus can last for hours, days or even weeks. Neither male nor female eats while it continues. If a female enters the spawning pool early, say in January, she will be grabbed instantly and is thereby sentenced to weeks of this embrace. The male's clasp is tight, and there seems little question that it must be uncomfortable as well as inconvenient. Many females are badly injured; some even die.

But there is more to amplexus than being on call to fertilise sperm. Amplexus is also exclusive. When a male frog is amplexed to a female, he is also asserting his right to fertilise her eggs. He is physically preventing any other males from getting access to them, whenever they might be laid.

This explains the free-for-all. Although amplexus looks firm and permanent, it relies merely on frog muscles to keep it going, and can thus be challenged and broken. Much of the unseemly writhing in a pond full of frogs stems from males trying to unseat their rivals and claim pole position on top of a female. Admittedly these challenges usually fail, but a male frog could find himself embraced in amplexus with a certain female for weeks and still lose his place at the last moment. Until those eggs come out, the fertilisation rights theoretically remain up for grabs.

Sometimes a displacement goes horribly wrong. Remember, a spawning pond tends to be a crowded, wild place, with sexual tension barely under control. If a male is displaced, this can sometimes trigger a mass brawl to get on top of a female, resulting in her death from drowning. But in common toads, and perhaps in common frogs as well, there can be a degree of 'negotiation' over amplexus. Scientists have discovered that large-bodied male toads, which can claim to be the healthier and higher quality individuals, have lower-pitched croaks than weedier, small-bodied toads. When an unmated male approaches a potential rival in amplexus, it croaks at it and the rival croaks back. If the incumbent has a suitably deep croak, it will probably be left alone, but if it betrays its vulnerability by croaking in a high-pitched voice an attack is much more likely to follow.

Of course female toads will also be listening closely to the croaking, because the quality of their own offspring is clearly at stake here, too. Most females will, of course, want to be coupled with a suitably high-quality male, so they will want their rider to be as deep-voiced as possible. Apparently some females collaborate in an unsuitable suitor's downfall: knowing that he will do badly in a croak-off, they swim off to that part of the pond most densely populated with toads to ensure that he is challenged and, with luck, displaced.

And if nothing else, this all simply proves that, much as frogs and toads need hugs to reproduce, there is no love lost in the hurly-burly of the spawning pond.

It Rains and it Blows

'WHY DON'T OWLS call in the rain?' goes the old schoolboy joke. 'Because it's too-wet-to-woo!' comes the triumphant reply. But little do the schoolboys know that behind this pun lies a sound biological truth.

Yes, tawny owls do call less often in the rain than on dry nights – this much had long been noticed by scientists, if not by budding comedians. Only recently, however, have they discovered the reason: it's all about transmission. Studies have discovered that the tawny owl's far-carrying hoot is only far-carrying on dry nights. In fact, it carries sixty-nine times better in the dry than in the wet. So the rain really does dampen the effectiveness of the message.

With snow and frost a diminishing issue by March, it is perhaps appropriate to consider the other kinds of inclement weather that our garden dwellers might experience. Both rain and wind are ever-present factors in many creatures' lives. But there has been a surprising lack of studies on how these less extreme forms of weather actually affect animals. Those that have been made are very revealing.

It turns out that, for our poor old owls, rain doesn't just muffle their hoot. It also restricts

their hunting. These hunters rely on hearing as much as sight to catch small mammals, and the rain often drowns out the telltale rustlings that reveal the whereabouts of their prey. So sometimes, unless they can find somewhere to shelter effectively, they just don't come out.

That, of course, makes wet nights a great bonus for small mammals. Without owls about, wood mice, bank voles and common shrews can all forage in peace. As a bonus for the shrews, the rain also brings earthworms to the surface, making them easy to find. This also helps the garden's other worm-hunters, such as hedgehogs, foxes and badgers.

Rain, in itself, is usually quite a benign force in the garden, unless it is prolonged or torrential, or both. Small flying invertebrates, such as mosquitoes, are apparently able to dodge the raindrops of even a downpour one by one, while larger invertebrates, such as butterflies, can usually take refuge among the grass or under leaves well in time to avoid problems. Caterpillars, on the other hand, are sometimes washed off leaves by torrential rain, leaving them in a spot of bother and with a long walk back. Although some insects must be struck by raindrops and washed away, the overall effect on their populations is not known.

Our larger garden animals tend to cope well with rain. Most birds spread waterproof oil over their plumage when preening, so water doesn't just run off a duck's back, but off any other bird's as well. Birds indeed often relish showers, bathing in and drinking from puddles, and sometimes flying through recently sodden leaves. Most mammals are equally well protected by their fur. Rain is a problem only when it makes food hard to find.

But what about wind? It transpires that worms, for their part, hate it. They need to leave their burrows to copulate (see page 30), but all sex is apparently cancelled when conditions are too windy. Mosquitoes, for all their immunity to raindrops, also greatly decrease in abundance and hatching when there is too much of a breeze, although on occasion these and other flying insects emerge preferentially in windy weather to

Raindrops: a deadly bombardment to a mosquito

Not the catch intended: water droplets on a web.

give them a head start in dispersing to new areas. One can only assume, though, that flying insects are generally not in favour of windy weather, and only travel – in those words of wisdom so familiar to all commuters – when their journeys are absolutely necessary.

As for vertebrates, most of us are bothered by the wind. In still conditions the bodies of both birds and mammals tend to retain a thin layer of insulating air adjacent to the skin, the so-called 'boundary layer', but its integrity is compromised by the wind – the mysterious 'wind-chill factor' so often mentioned in weather reports. The fur of mammals and the feathers of birds are usually streamlined in one direction. So when, for example, a fox turns its back to the wind, the air ruffles its fur and gets into the boundary layer, making the fox uncomfortable. This explains why flocks of birds such as gulls always face into the wind.

Wind also has a metabolic effect. In small animals in particular, metabolic rate increases in the wind, partly because of the lowered temperature but partly, no doubt, because of the need to work against the wind physically. Such creatures therefore use up more oxygen and, in consequence, it is hardly surprising that they tend to look for shelter when there is a strong breeze outside. A good many animals are physically affected by the wind when they hunt or forage for food. Birds and squirrels, for example, tend to stay lower in the trees when there is a strong wind blowing.

Finally, of course, the wind can muck up the transmission of sounds just as much as the rain can, as anyone who has had to shout to a friend across a windy street instinctively knows. Sometimes this can have serious and immediate consequences, for example when an animal is unable to hear an alarm call made by another and falls prey to a predator it might otherwise have avoided. Similarly, birds making contact calls might, in theory at least, be more easily separated from one another during windy or rainy conditions.

At this time of the year wind can also blow away songs. And this, I'm afraid, brings us back to our owl again. Not only does the rain quash his hoot, which must be bad enough, but now the breeze gusts it away, too. It is simply, as the schoolboy might say, 'too windy to woo'!

Looks like it's going to be a long night in for this tawny owl.

The Underworld of Moles

MOLES ARE TOO pesky to be popular and too weird to be loved, but there can be few quite such extraordinary creatures in any garden. They are our only truly fossorial mammals, which means that they live almost entirely underground, burrowing through the soil for a living and rarely seeing the light of day. Plenty of invertebrates exist like this – earthworms, for instance – but the mole is alone among our furry or feathered animals in following such an extreme subterranean lifestyle.

March is a big month for moles, since it heralds the beginning of their breeding season. This brings with it a challenge, forcing moles to break out of their comfort zone. And when you lie settled in your own tunnel system for much of the year, as moles do, with everything you need on tap, the temptation must be to stay exactly as you are and let the breeding season pass you by.

After all, the only thing that moles seem to lack in their burrows is a TV set. All individuals live in a system of corridors about 5cm wide and 4cm high, which leads to a larger chamber that contains the nest. The dimensions of the tunnels correspond to those of the moles, so if a mole is travelling one way and wishes to retrace its steps, it must either start moving backwards or it does a roll, nose-first, rather like a competition swimmer coming to the end of a length.

One beauty of this life is that a mole need not travel far to find food. The burrows themselves act as pitfall traps for a variety of vagabond invertebrates, and a wandering mole need only collect what has fallen from the walls or ceiling. To help it to detect prey in the complete darkness of the underground network (burrows can be anything from flush to the surface to 70cm down), a mole has both an

exceedingly sensitive nose and an impressive growth of whiskers. Its sharp teeth do the rest.

So the only real effort required in a mole's life is when constructing the tunnel system in the first place. This, of course, involves a great deal of digging, but the mole is highly efficient at this, being able to shift twice its own weight of soil in a single minute. It uses its massive front paws, each fitted with ferocious-looking claws, to make progress, each front limb working alternately in a kind of hybrid between the breast-stroke and the front crawl. The displaced soil, of course, has to go somewhere, and unfortunately it ends up as a molehill – a source of much aggravation for farmers and gardeners, and often the only clue that there are moles about. The final length of the burrow system is dependent on the abundance of available food: as a rule, the longer the tunnel, the poorer the soil. In good areas the tunnels may only add up to 70m; in other places, 150m.

For much of the year moles lead a very solitary life. Their burrows are single units, which the owners mark with urine at intervals to keep intruders away. If boundaries are crossed, fights take place, for the tunnel is both home and foraging ground for every owner, making it a patch well worth defending. Intriguingly, however, while the tunnel network of an individual might be exclusive, the actual home range of each mole – the area of ground in which its system lies – might be shared with others. In other words, tunnels

Earth star: resting its huge, clawed arms, a mole takes a break.

Here comes trouble: moles don't mix well, and a chance meeting often triggers a fight.

might criss-cross through an area, but not be connected. Individuals that have been tracked have a tendency to rest in the furthest point in their network from where their neighbours are residing, rather like our tendency on tube trains to stand or sit as far away from the others in the carriage as possible. Clearly, they know all about their neighbours' activities – who is going out with whom, whose tunnel is vacant, who has babies, and so on. It is not hard to imagine them holding a cup to their walls and listening in on private conversations.

However, as mentioned above, this cosy solo existence is interrupted every year by the necessity of breeding. And in order to find one another underground, moles simply resort to what they know best: they dig. Or at least, the males do. They extend their burrow system outwards and, in so doing, invade the home ranges of neighbouring females. While on the hunt they may stray from their nest for days at a time, sleeping uncomfortably in a burrow. Once they reach a receptive partner, they quickly mate. This may be the last time they meet, and it is the one and only occasion on which an encounter between two moles in a tunnel does not turn nasty.

The breeding season of moles, as mentioned above, tends to begin in March. However, in

northern parts of Europe it may start as late as May and in the Mediterranean region as early as January. At first there seems to be nothing strange about having such a flexible arrangement, but then you wonder: how do the moles know what season of the year it is? After all, they live entirely underground.

The evidence suggests that the breeding season in moles is probably triggered, as in so many animals, by the increasing length of the day. And it is certainly true that moles can see light, just about, and that they do sometimes come above ground to collect bedding material. But surely one of the very strangest aspects of the life of this strange creature is this: although it lives beneath the soil, its life is governed by the sun.

You can't miss mole activity in grassland, but in woodland molehills go almost unnoticed.

APRIL IS A month in a hurry. The leaves don't just open out, they burst out; the early flowers, such as daffodils, disappear with indecorous speed, like an out-of-fashion range in a department store, to be replaced by the seasonal blooms. And meanwhile, the train of reproduction is careering down the track, with most of the garden's wildlife on board, as creatures seek to exploit the best breeding conditions of the year.

APRIL

The Breeding Bandwagon

'Up a bit…no, down a bit': a collared dove preens its mate.

IF YOU WERE to take a straw-poll of all the garden animals during April and ask them what was their most important task at that moment, the chances are that just about all of them would offer the same reply: breeding. For some this would simply mean 'preparing for breeding'; for others 'actually breeding'; and the rest would be too busy to reply, because they would already be embroiled in the maelstrom of parenting. The fact is that spring is the key season in the reproduction of just about everything.

Few larger animals would fit the first category, although there would be plenty of invertebrates. The only real laggards among mammals are bats, which are often still asleep throughout much of April. They aren't taking A-levels or following degrees, though; it's just that the season for flying insects is yet to come and there isn't enough consistently available food to keep their fuel-hungry engines running.

The same story applies to a few of our garden birds. Two of them, the spotted flycatcher and the swift, don't even arrive in this country until the end of the month or even in May. Swifts spend most of their lives flying in the sky and catching small creatures that do the same, such as aphids,

so they rely on settled, warm weather to generate good food supplies and, ultimately, fuel an attempt at breeding. The flycatchers rely for their food on the larger insects of the garden, such as bluebottles, which tend to appear later on. The sparrowhawk, our commonest garden bird of prey, also delays its breeding to exploit a particular food supply. This species wants its eggs to hatch when there are plenty of young birds, such as tits, leaving their nests and fluttering around with near-suicidal incompetence. It therefore lays its eggs in May.

For many garden animals, April is a time taken up with either searching for a mate or trying to beguile this newfound member of the opposite sex. Again, it is often birds that exhibit this most clearly. Woodpigeons and collared doves, for example, often sit side by side on rooftops and preen each other shamelessly. Crows often do the same, and while doing so they whisper sweet nothings to one another in a language all their own, without the usual harsh, spiteful cawing. Other birds are less demonstrative, but the sight of one robin, for example, often leads to the other, as the two stick together in nuptial bliss. Indeed, at this time of the year males of many

species, including robins and tits, bring regular offerings of food for their mates, which the latter accept with a display similar to that of a young bird begging. But this is 'courtship feeding', a way for the male to sustain the female through her tough schedule of egg production, relieving her of the need to find all her food for herself.

Meanwhile, there are many fresh liaisons taking place. Most butterflies, for example, have typically only just hatched out so, to get their breeding programme underway, they will spend much of their time on sunny days searching for a mate. Once initial contact has been made (see page 56), they then have to engage patiently and fastidiously in what can be a long and careful courtship ritual. Essentially, the male butterfly takes its female to a quiet spot where the couple are unlikely to be disturbed – often in the evening. Then it faces the female and flutters its wings in exactly the right way to keep her juices flowing, wafting pheromones towards her to enhance her mood. In some butterflies the male will actually enclose the female's antennae with his wings, making sure that she is almost overpowered by the chemical aphrodisiacs produced on their surface. Little by little, the butterflies dance and exchange chemical signals until, at last, the female lifts her wings invitingly and they mate.

The courtship of hedgehogs, by contrast, lies at the other end of the choreography spectrum. These animals, it turns out, are about as refined in matters of love as, let's say, two eunuch hippopotamuses with indigestion. The male approaches a feeding female and, without a shred of subtlety, snorts a bit as if to say: "How about it, missus?" Understandably, she reacts by keeping her rear end well out of reach and, in return, also snorts or puffs, using words that cannot decently be printed here. Heedless of this rebuff, the male begins to circle the female with a view to trying it on anyway, and the female rejects his advances again. This may go on for hours, and sometimes just peters out when one suitor wearily leaves the arena. Other males may also turn up, interrupting the efforts of the first male and sometimes usurping him. But eventually, after a lot of huffing and puffing, the female's house is finally blown down. Mating is difficult and ungainly, though the female flattens her spines to make things a little less hazardous for the male.

Hedgehog mating is noisy, ungainly and potentially perilous.

Newt choreography

For a little more more dash and class, look in the shallows of a well-vegetated garden pond, where newts will delight you by demonstrating their flashy courtship routines. In contrast to frogs and toads, in which males claim females by jumping on top of them and hugging them in the amplexus position (*see page 40*), newts must use guile and style to earn the opportunity to reproduce, and throughout the course of their elaborate displays a single mistake can undermine the entire effort, with the female quickly losing interest and swimming away. Each male also has to distract his potential mate's attention from rivals, so his display has to be pretty impressive.

Looks aren't everything among newts, but they do help. In spring, males of all our three species – the smooth, palmate and crested newts – develop bright orangey colours on the underside and tail, and acquire crests along their upper surface, which they show off to the females. Studies have shown that a female, inevitably, pays more attention to males with relatively large crests. But, happily, display skills do count for something and so, crucially, does chemistry.

A male must first position himself in front of the female, at a slightly curious angle, so that she roughly faces his tail while he seems to be peering behind her to see whether her tail is still attached. This, it transpires, is the ideal pose from which to waft chemical pheromones towards her, using a quivering motion and theatrical shakes of his colourful tail. He then leads her on something of a dance, continually repositioning himself and quivering until, with his object of affection saturated by his pheromone aphrodisiacs and dazzled by his ballet, he finally delivers a small capsule full of sperm in front of her. If all goes well, she manoeuvres forward a bit, guided by the male, until the spermatophore is directly beneath her cloaca, whereupon it attaches itself and passes into her reproductive tract.

After such a long and precise courtship, it is perhaps not surprising that newts eschew the rather careless mass production practised by frogs and toads. After fertilisation, the female only lays a couple of hundred eggs, as opposed to several thousand, and she laboriously and lovingly wraps each one individually in a leaf of aquatic vegetation. This protects them both from predators and from the sun's ultraviolet rays.

In smooth newt courtship, the male dazzles the female with colour and motion and drugs her with aphrodisiac.

Another tadpole meets its end in the jaws of a water boatman.

Hatching out

The female newt's parental responsibilities end with wrapping up her eggs. In garden birds, however, the adult remains with the eggs until they hatch and beyond, both warming and protecting them by applying body heat from a patch of bare skin on the belly. This process is known to us all as incubation, and is much more active and energy-sapping than many people realise. Parent birds are constantly turning eggs around underneath them, to ensure that heat is distributed evenly through the clutch and also to prevent any part of the yolk sticking to the shell. Adult birds also tend to take regular breaks in incubation to feed and refresh themselves, sometimes as frequently as every twenty minutes or so.

Just about every garden bird species will be on eggs at some time in April. On average a female blue tit or great tit, for example, will have begun to lay in the first week of the month, although this does depend partly on the weather leading up to the event. Equally, such birds as carrion crows, robins, blackbirds and dunnocks can also be found sitting, whether the nest is a fortress in the treetops or a barely visible cup on the side of a bank.

Meanwhile, back at the pond, some eggs are unmistakably hatching, taking reproduction to the next phase. Those eggs laid by frogs and toads last month have now become tadpoles, the larval stage between egg and juvenile (an intermediate persona lacking in birds). Once tadpoles appear in ponds, it soon becomes clear why frogs and toads lay so many eggs, because eating these long-tailed blobs seems to be something of a rite of passage for every aquatic creature imaginable. This is partly because tadpoles are pretty defenceless and gormless and partly because they make a splendidly nutritious snack. The tadpoles themselves graze on algae and the occasional bit of dead meat. But, seemingly inevitably, they soon become the latter themselves: everything from moorhen to water boatman sinks bill, teeth or mouthparts into them at intervals so regular that it seems impossible any should survive. Indeed, their three-month development under water would doubtless be a time of claustrophobic terror, were the tadpoles not so blissfully unaware of their peril.

There must be something about being a larva. Up on the trees or among the grass, caterpillars, the larvae of butterflies and moths, are similarly maltreated – well OK, eaten – by almost everything. Although only a few species are at large in April, those that have appeared are often super-abundant (*see page 54*) so that a single family of tits, for example, can take about 10,000 in a couple of weeks with no effect on the overall productivity of the particular caterpillar species. This constitutes disposable, mass production of what is a very simple product: a crawling tube with jaws.

Not all larvae are quite so quiescent, of course. Some are violent and predatory in this early stage, so much so that one fears how they will turn out as adults. The larvae of ladybirds, for example, destroy aphids more quickly than a school kid zaps enemies on a Playstation, while dragonfly larvae, with their terrible jaws, lie in the mud at the bottom of the pond or stay concealed in the aquatic vegetation, and ambush prey with ruthless efficiency. Indeed the latter are

A sight to stir and terrify: the dragonfly larva is a voracious predator at the bottom of the pond.

so nimble that, should they miss with their initial attempt, they can often strike again before their target has time to get away. True to form, these hunters later progress from being hitmen of the pond to fully-fledged assassins of the sky.

Mammals don't have a larval stage, nor – except for some Australian oddities – an external egg stage. So, perhaps it is not surprising that it is among some of our mammals that breeding is most advanced in April. Badgers were first off the mark, giving birth to cubs in February, with foxes and squirrels not far behind. For these mammals, an early start means that their young will take their first steps into the garden when it is at its most benign and productive. Even so, parent mammals remain highly protective: fox and badger cubs just about make it to the entrance of the earth or sett and look out with tentative curiosity, while young squirrels come out only briefly and under strict parental curfew.

April also signals the start of the breeding season for most of the smallest mammals in the garden, namely mice, voles and shrews. The territorial arrangements are set up before breeding actually starts, and mating can be under way by the beginning of the month, or even earlier. Gestation only takes about 20 days, so it is perfectly possible for the youngsters to be born in the same month they were conceived. Thus these small, highly productive mites can quickly catch up with the larger mammals, despite their slow start. Breeding is a bandwagon: they jump on it eagerly and are soon travelling fast.

The First Cuckoo of Spring

IT CAN SAFELY be said that, much as human listeners might eagerly anticipate hearing the first cuckoo of spring, with the chance of a letter in *The Times* and a place in the record books, the same does not go for the garden's small bird community. In fact, the cuckoo is quite a rare sight in gardens these days, even rural ones, but that does not diminish its impact on the small bird psyche. Even a fleeting visit from a cuckoo in transit will bring furious mock attacks from host species, who quickly recognise the intruder and try to speed it on its way – like angry middle-Englanders confronting members of the travelling community. The cuckoo, much as it has declined, can still get right under a small bird's skin.

The reason, of course, is so well known as to be proverbial. The cuckoo is a rare example of a brood parasite, a bird that contracts out the rearing of its young to unknowing and unwilling clients, without paying for any upkeep. Indeed,

it is the host parents who pay. The young cuckoo hatches ridiculously early, having obtained a head start in life by developing unusually well within the female cuckoo's oviduct, and it soon commits its fellow clutch or brood members to an early grave by shoving them over the side of the nest and to the oblivion of the cruel ground below. Having secured its position as the only nest occupant, free of competition, it soon grows obscenely large and beseeches its foster parents to redouble their efforts on every visit by imitating the cries of a desperately hungry nestling. Having milked the efforts of its unwitting carers, it will then, if it is a female, return the following year and concentrate its efforts on parasitising the very species whose tender care brought it into the world. It is a fine example of how some individuals always manage to bypass the system.

The male's part in all this is very limited, but it is he who provides the species' signature two-note song – perhaps the only bird sound that just

Cuckoos are unwelcome wherever they go.

about everyone can recognise. Or can they? In the old days, arriving cuckoos were sometimes heard as early as the end of February, but such a possibility has diminished now and any song by mid-April would still be from an impressively early bird. So what should we make of any claims from earlier in the year? It would make sense to assume that some, especially if they were faint and distant, might actually hail from the collared dove, a bird with a song of similar pitch. Even experts can be confused by muffled birds, so we should treat any modern record-breaking claims with caution.

However, there are some cuckoos that are still common in our gardens today, if only we knew it, and they usually arrive in April or even earlier. These cuckoos don't look much like the birds, and they don't sound like them, either. They buzz. These cuckoos are bees.

Cuckoo bees don't take their name from their appearance. They get it from their devious habits. Just like the birds after which they are named, these insects are parasites. And they are just as sneaky, and ultimately just as destructive to their hosts, as any feathered perpetrators.

To understand how cuckoo bees operate, we also need to appreciate the workings of their colony of hosts, which will consist of bumblebees of a certain species. After 'hibernating' during the winter months, a queen bumblebee founds a colony by laying eggs from sperm it stored in the autumn. These eggs hatch into worker bees, which are, empirically, its daughters, although they are also very much underlings. A worker bee's job is, as in most bee colonies, to collect nectar to feed everybody and pollen to nourish the growing larvae from eggs laid by the queen. At first the queen's new eggs simply replenish the supply of workers, which die off regularly, but as the summer progresses some of the new eggs eventually hatch into new queens, and also males. Males fertilise new queens, and the latter overwinter and form the nucleus for next year's generation.

From the cuckoo bee's point of view, the weak point in the bumblebee's lifecycle is at the beginning, when the queen has hatched the first batch of workers in the early spring. Cuckoo bees rouse from hibernation about three weeks after their hosts, and they soon set about looking for vulnerable colonies. Once they have selected one, they creep up unnoticed and mingle with the workers, like assassins in the crowd. Crucially, they become smothered in the specific chemicals that coat the colony, thus cloaking their identity. Very soon all the rich resources of the collective – their food, their nest and their workforce – will be ready for a takeover. All the parasite must do is neutralise the queen.

Cuckoo bees are generally larger than their hosts, and they are primed for the fight. The subsequent coup is often violent, and the host queen frequently killed. That is not unusual in bumblebee society, because queens that have failed to found a colony will also sometimes take one by force. However, this time the winner is both a different species and a professional parasite.

The death of the host queen means that no more workers will be produced, because cuckoo bees don't make workers, they simply appropriate them. All the cuckoo queen does now is to feed heartily on the food brought to her by her new underlings, lay eggs of her own species, and watch the host workers bring up her progeny. The only survivors from the colony will be the overwintering queens of the cuckoo bee. It is that simple.

Not everything in the animal kingdom is quite what it seems and, just as in human society, there always seem to be those who try to cheat the system, so it is in the wilds of the garden. Next time you need to talk about the birds and the bees, remember what your mother did not tell you.

Battle of the bees: a cuckoo bee (right) makes its deadly challenge.

Tits and Caterpillars

IT'S APRIL, AND the feeding stations provided for our birds are probably largely quiet by now. The hanging seed-hoppers are empty of customers after five months of constant use, and the visitors to our bird table no longer need to queue for a perch. Something has happened, especially to our blue and great tits. We might still have greenfinches guzzling away on the feeders like workmen chewing their sandwiches, but much of the liveliness, colour and glamour has faded from the scene.

The reason is simple: this is the time when the blue tits and great tits we know so well have, quite frankly, received a better offer. They have moved up in life – to the treetops. The leaf-buds are opening and these reveal caterpillars, the great annual food fad of blue tits and many other birds. The spring brings a glut of these larvae, and they are, in many ways, the perfect nutrition: abundant, easy to find, pretty helpless, and healthy eating. Never mind our five-a-day fruit and veg allocation: with caterpillars, it's hundreds a day, for everyone.

The caterpillar glut affects the tits in profound ways. For a start, they time their breeding season so that, when the young hatch, the supply of food is at its peak. And, even more profoundly, the glut means that it is expedient for the birds to place, quite literally, all their eggs into one annual basket. Most small garden bird species have a long breeding season, during which they might attempt to raise several families of youngsters. Tits, by contrast, aim to raise just one family a year. But it is a very big one: blue tits often have more than ten eggs in a clutch.

That, of course, is a lot of young mouths to feed all at once, and it gives some idea of just how large a glut of caterpillars is required. At the height of the season, the parent tits may bring 1,000 caterpillars a day to their hungry youngsters, although several hundred is more usual. How does the caterpillar population survive this onslaught? The answer appears to be fairly easily. It has been estimated that, in a good year, a really big tree of the most caterpillar-friendly species, the oak, may hold half a million. Even the less well-endowed trees may yield 1,000 caterpillars for every square-metre vertical column over the tree's extent. So, if all goes well, nobody will go without.

Of course, this is all fine if the birds get their timing right. But if they don't, disaster is almost unavoidable. The peak season for the caterpillar bonanza described above is often very short, perhaps no more than a couple of weeks, so if the birds start to lay their eggs late for any reason, or too early, they could miss this peak and consequently struggle. Equally, the caterpillar glut is not always at the same time each year; it varies in intensity as well.

Food on a string: caterpillars on their threads make easy prey for a blue tit.

So there are a number of things that can go wrong. You can often tell when the tits are having a bad time by the food they bring to their chicks. If it comprises plenty of caterpillars, that's a good sign; if other insects besides caterpillars, things may be dodgy but not disastrous. If the birds attempt to feed artificial food to the young, such as fare from the bird table, it probably means that things are bad. In recent years there has been much debate about whether to feed birds in the summer, mainly triggered by some old observations of tit nestlings dying by choking on nuts. The scare misses the point: if a parent tit is trying to feed such stuff to its young, they are already on borrowed time.

It is easy to forget, when the fortunes of blue and great tits grab our attention, that there are other matters of survival at stake here, too. What about the caterpillars themselves? They didn't come into being just for the purpose of providing snacks for tits, but have a life and a survival strategy of their own. What is the point of their populations exploding over such a short time?

Several interpretations have been made of this spring glut. One is that the caterpillars flood the market over a brief period so that the predation will be set only at a level that the tits are adapted to over the course of a year, and no more. Another, rather more prosaic explanation, is that the caterpillars come out for the same reason that the tits do: a glut of food. In the case of the most numerous of the tits' prey species and the best-studied tree, the winter moth and oak respectively, it seems that the oak leaves are at their most nutritious when they have just unfolded. Their nitrogen and water content are at their highest, and the levels of tannin, a protein that may both stiffen leaves and deter predators like caterpillars, are at their lowest. The caterpillars, therefore, are also timing their emergence carefully.

And, as in the case of the tits, it can go wrong. Oaks and other trees are fickle and individually variable, and the caterpillars, which hatch from eggs that might have been laid by adult moths as long ago as December, could easily emerge to find that the leaves haven't yet burst. When this happens they have just hours to live, and many perish. But to cope with this dire emergency they spin a thread that acts like a parachute and allow the wind to whisk them to another tree elsewhere. This might be a different species, but as long as it has fresh leaves, they are saved. If all goes well and the caterpillars avoid predation,

they eventually spin another line of silk and let themselves down to the ground, where they pupate and then emerge in the late autumn.

Thus, the lives and fortunes of tits and caterpillars are neatly interwoven. Before leaving this subject, one interesting and frequently-asked question remains: why do adult tits always bring

Room service: parent blue tits have to work hard to feed their mass-produced nestlings.'

just one caterpillar at a time to their young, whereas other small birds bring whole batches of wiggly worms or flies? The answer, quite simply, is that caterpillars aren't quite as helpless as I may have suggested above. They bite. So, as the parent tit brings the caterpillar to its young, it has to break its jaws by bashing it on a hard surface, otherwise it might injure or choke the nestling. This is much easier to do with just a single caterpillar in the bill.

The Spiral Pathway

APRIL IS THAT time of year when the garden at last begins to bloom with butterflies, those fragile insects that flicker inoffensively around like motorised petals of blossom. They are part of the eye-candy of spring and summer, each a little tribute to fair weather. It is easy to sentimentalise thoughts of butterflies, and many creative writers have done just this, dreaming them into a magical, utopian garden landscape in the company of hopping bunnies and squirrels that talk. Unfortunately this presupposes a gentleness and mildness in a butterfly's character that simply isn't there. The reality of these vibrant insects is that they, like the rest of us, are hot-tempered and red-blooded. Butterflies might look peace-loving and fragile, but the only real fragility is in the state of relations between them.

In fact, the world of the butterfly is a highly competitive one. The insect's primary motivation can be summed up by a study showing that the average adult male butterfly actually spends more of its lifetime seeking or consorting with the opposite sex than it spends feeding. In other words, it doesn't seek sex between meals, but rather the other way around.

It only takes a moment of observation in the garden to confirm that something is going on. If you spend enough time watching butterflies it won't be long before you see two that are apparently buffeting each other in mid-air, twirling around like two boxers in a ring. This will usually be a contest between two males, and there is a fair chance that they will be jousting over rights to a territory. In butterfly society, the ownership of territory is the way to get ahead.

In most species, butterfly territories are very small. In the speckled wood, a very common species that favours shady gardens, it may constitute no more than a patch of bright sunlight and is seldom larger than 14m². In the peacock, some individuals of which will have emerged recently from hibernation, it is likely to be a herbaceous

Speckled and dappled: two rival male speckled woods fighting over territory.

border or one side of the garden, amounting to no more than a maximum total of 50m². Interestingly, speckled woods often occupy their territories in the morning before taking a break, while peacocks usually spend the morning feeding and basking, only taking up their territories in the afternoon. But whenever it is on station, the territory holder's primary task is watching the world go by.

Sometimes the traffic that passes is very welcome, especially when it takes the nubile form of a receptive female. Her appearance, indeed, is why males hold a territory in the first place, and they take pains to defend a spot where a female is most likely to pass, attracted by sun or flowers. When such a visitor shows up, the males eagerly investigate the object of their interest, and will gleefully abandon their territory as they flirt away in the sunshine. However, the visitor is sometimes a rival male, intent upon disruption, in which case the behaviour of the incumbent male is very different.

Just about every gardener must have seen a tussle between two speckled woods. One individual flies normally on its way, when suddenly another appears from below and intercepts it. The two then knock wings and, as if engaged in one of the more vigorous Latin dances, spiral rapidly upwards together, bumping into one another as they go. The scene is often framed within a shaft of sunlight, like a dramatic spotlit moment in a darkened theatre. The feud ends when the rivals reach some mutually agreed height, whereupon both fly off in separate directions, with the territory-holding male almost invariably returning to his perch, and the intruder disappearing over the garden fence, somewhat chastened, like a guilty driver leaving the scene after receiving a speeding ticket.

The odd part of the procedure is the result. The winner of this tussle is almost always the male that is already in the driving seat – the current owner of the territory. Very occasionally there is a displacement, when perhaps the original owner is not up to the task, but this happens so rarely that one wonders what the whole palaver is actually for. Only sometimes, when the butterflies are well matched, or when a territory-holding male returns to its perch after a skirmish and finds a usurper has sneaked in, do the battles last for more than a few seconds or spill away from the territory. But even in these cases, the original owner always seems to win.

Equally intriguing, at least in the case of the speckled wood, is that territory-holding is by no means universal among the given males in a local colony and is not the sole pathway to finding a female. Males can also try 'patrolling', which is just a big word for flying about, looking in likely places and hoping to come across a female.

A male holly blue living up to its name.

Individuals, in fact, will routinely divide their time between a spot of territory-holding in the morning and patrolling in the afternoon. Interestingly, there is a correlation between the behaviour of individuals with different colouration: paler-hued speckled woods spend more time on territories, while darker individuals are more likely to devote their time to patrolling. This is thought to relate to the fact that darker wings absorb heat from the sun more quickly than paler wings, enabling the latter group to spend more time flying about.

Not all butterfly species even bother with spaced out territories. Male holly blues tend to gather together around a high hedge of ivy and form a haze of blue to which females are attracted, coming from some distance to check out the holly blue hullabaloo. Once there, they can presumably choose from the many males present.

But the holly blue is something of an exception, and males of most species of butterfly strike out on their own. No blood is spilt on the spiral pathway, but the tension is there for all to see.

MAY IS THE height of vibrant spring: colourful and refreshing, busy and bright. Few of the garden's animals have escaped its summons, as they race to find mates and reproduce. But not all of them go about breeding in the conventional fashion. This month of the year, as much as any other, holds a few surprises.

MAY

Gender Agendas

IN THE HURLY-BURLY of spring, the urge to reproduce holds sway over almost all our garden animals. Many have short lives and must do everything in their power to pass their genes on as quickly as possible. Furthermore, the season is short, and sometimes animals must cut corners and cross boundaries to get the job done. The result is that, sadly, things are not always pretty. In our human lives – at least in western culture – we generally agree that families do best when the two sexes stick to an exclusive pair bond. In some animals this is the case, too. For many creatures, however, and very many more than you might expect, the idea of keeping to a single partner makes no sense. There is simply too much at stake genetically to risk being committed to what might be a duff mate.

Among garden wildlife, therefore, there exists a continuum of reproductive behaviour. It ranges from exclusive pair bonds at one end to rampant promiscuity at the other, and includes some arrangements that completely overturn our ideas of gender. Many of our most familiar garden ani-mals occupy surprising places on this continuum. But of course, in a garden full of secrets, unlikely liaisons often make for the juiciest gossip.

For many garden vertebrates, our hallowed human system of long-term monogamy simply doesn't work. The main problem is that, although many birds and mammals do indeed play distinct roles within family life and have a strong practical pair bond as a framework, the genetic dimension to their relationship is quite different. For example, it had always been assumed that foxes, which are highly territorial creatures, were monogamous, with the dominant male responsible for fathering all the cubs in a litter. However, it transpires that this is far from always the case – at least in dense populations. The subdominant males, if present in a social group, may also sire cubs, and even foxes from other groups may contribute their genetic material. This is extraordinary for two reasons: first, male foxes from neighbouring groups are risking serious injury by trespassing into their neighbours' territories at a time of great tension; second, a female fox is only

This idyllic scene may not be all it seems: the cubs may not all share the same father.

Swallow chicks beg for food from their parents. But do they know who their father is?

fertile for three days in a year, which is exactly when – as you would expect – the dominant male becomes unusually attentive to her.

However, these extra-pair couplings certainly take place and the reason is pretty clear: when a female and male are in a stable relationship there is a guarantee of shared parental care, so it pays to uphold this arrangement; if one of the pair is weak, however, or if there are attractive members of the opposite sex available close at hand, a few liaisons on the side may well produce one or more fitter, healthier offspring.

The same considerations apply to many of our garden birds. In recent years many of our most familiar species, including blue and great tits, house sparrows, starlings and swallows, have all been exposed as regular 'love rats', routinely cheating on their partners. The two sexes are equally culpable, and some species show a greater tendency towards multiple mates than others. Swallows, in particular, seem quite unable to resist the charms of the opposite sex, especially when all the locals live in colonies and may have nests rather close to each other. It so happens that female swallows can readily assess the quality of a partner: the longer and more symmetrical his two tail-streamers, the more desirable the male and thus the more likely he is to father a great many more chicks 'on the side'. So, presumably, it must be hard for female swallows to resist such visible temptation.

Several of our mammal species dispense entirely with the formality of pairing up to breed and instead are genuinely promiscuous. This occurs mainly in those in which the female is

perfectly capable of raising the brood herself without any help from a male. Thus hedgehogs, squirrels and bats are free to copulate with any partner they choose, and won't have any explaining to do when they return home. Observations of hedgehogs have revealed that a female may have 12 different mates over two seasons, and a male may go through the courtship rigmarole ten times over the same period. Meanwhile, a female squirrel usually mates with only two or three males for each litter, but the males tend to be more promiscuous than this.

A few garden birds take the sharing of mates to a more formal level, becoming bigamous or polygamous. In these relationships there is a real pair bond that lasts for much of the breeding period, it's just that a given individual has two mates rather than one. Male wrens, for example, quite commonly have two female partners, each with its own nest and each demanding help from the father in the form of defending the territory and, ideally, feeding the young. But the most extreme example of sharing mates comes from one of the garden's more self-effacing characters, the dunnock. This small bird exhibits an unprecedented variety of options for a breeding adult. Many pairs are monogamous, but it is very common for a female to have relations with two or three mates simultaneously. Less often a male manages to keep two females to himself, and very occasionally three. And, just to stir the brew, sometimes a triangle becomes a square, in that a male sharing a female with another male also acquires another female for himself; so now both sexes are sharing.

One of the reasons for this behaviour in dunnocks is that, by copulating with a female, a male is effectively signing an agreement to help feed and raise the resulting young. Dunnocks deliver many tiny food items to their young, and often require a team in order to do the job effectively. So it is expedient for females to allow a number of males to mount her: she can thus enlist them into the task force.

Best of both worlds

For some garden creatures, there is no chance of illicit hanky-panky. This is because each one carries the organs of both sexes within its body, so it is impossible for male and female to keep any secrets from one another: they are joined at the hip – and pretty much everywhere else. This

Two male dunnocks (below) square up to each other with the 'wing-waving' display. Meanwhile, a third male (left) is about to join in.

arrangement ensures that each individual finds a ready-made partner in every other individual it meets. Thus many of the garden's hermaphrodites are creatures that move slowly: worms, snails and slugs, for example. Living in the crawler lane means that they tend to bump into others of their species rather less often than speedier animals do. But the beauty is that when they do, the stranger in question is bound to be a perfect match.

It is easy to think of snails as being like a couple who live in a caravan. They crawl along in their own self-contained little world, happily oblivious to the rest of life (and probably holding up the traffic). Yet if this impression suggests a lack of passion, think again. When one snail meets another, the two simply fizz with lust. Copulation may continue for hours on end and, having had their way with one partner, each quite frequently does much the same with the very next one it meets. Summer nights can be long and exhausting.

The courtship of snails is complex and protracted. At first it is easy to appreciate what is going on: the two snails begin with a tender touching of the tentacles and quickly proceed to what can only be described as 'kissing', as they rear up slightly on their soles and make mouth-to-mouth contact. But the parallels with us quickly disappear as the two snails start to release copious mucus to ease the next stage of the ritual. They then lie side by side until eventually the sexual organs are everted. It may now take hours for the two sets to engage and the sperms to be transferred from one to the other in their little capsules,

called spermatophores. Indeed, this may happen long after the apparent ardour has subsided and the two snails are, metaphorically, smoking their post-coital cigarettes.

Perhaps the most intriguing part of this ritual, however, occurs when the snails first make genital-to-genital contact. And it is one of those aspects of animal behaviour that, were it not incontestably true, you might be sorely tempted to dismiss as nonsense. If you ever find a pair of snails in close contact, which you sometimes can on fine, dewy mornings in spring and summer, look out for small white, chalky shards embedded in their flesh. These, astonishingly, are 'love-darts', made up from proteins and calcium carbonate, which the animals propel at each other in the midst of their courtship. Their exact function remains disputed by scientists, but they appear to be critical to the whole process: if a snail fires and misses, or the dart does not embed correctly, the procedure slows down considerably. And, let's face it, it cannot be a good idea to slow down a snail. It seems probable that the darts help the timing of the procedure and may add an element of spice

– though some suggest that its real function is actually to inhibit immediate sexual relations once the animals have parted.

Worms, too, are hermaphrodites, and their mating rituals also have a certain charm and intrigue. There is certainly an agreeably bashful element at the start, when the worms come creeping out of their burrows like naughty schoolboys heading for the girls' dormitories. Actually their reticence is all about the ever-present threat of being gobbled up, because mating worms are extremely vulnerable to their extensive list of predators. If the coast is clear, a worm will stretch out from the soil towards a nearby worm that has the same idea and, guided by scent and good vibrations, the two soon make thrilling tactile contact.

Two snails meet, albeit somewhat bashfully. This is really a meeting of two couples, since snails have both male and female organs in the same body.

Things are hotting up as one snail fires its 'love-dart' onto the other's flesh.

They lie side by side, with their backward-pointing bristles providing some friction as their bodies touch, while at the same time each worm keeps its tail lodged in the burrow entrance, in case of danger. Again mucus casts a veil over the proceedings, effectively taping the two together in a head-to-toe embrace. Just like snails, the partners may stay together for hours, during which time the sperm is transferred. Eventually, job done, they return to the soil.

Some smaller garden creatures can reproduce without any sex at all, and their populations are dominated by one gender – invariably the female. Take the aphids that we gardeners admire so much when we find them on our runner beans: they are all female. Aphids – which, technically speaking, are bugs – build up their summer populations by a system called parthenogenesis, which entails females giving virgin birth to females. The babies are genetic clones of their mother. And they aren't babies for long, either: the little darlings can reproduce, by the same method, within a fortnight. Parthenogenesis removes that awkward need to find a mate and allows aphid populations to explode when there is plenty of food, which is vital for their survival. Aphids, after all, are about as defenceless as an animal gets; they rely on sheer numbers to swamp their losses.

There are such things as male aphids, but these are almost an afterthought. In late summer, when the females have made their presence felt on their favoured plants, the changing weather triggers the aphids to produce males and egg-laying females. These new males seek out the females and mate, and the eggs they fertilise sit out the winter to become the next generation in spring.

Girl power: these aphids are all females, males being a late-summer rarity.

Little prickles: when they grow up, these young hedgehogs may have 5,000 spines – about twice the number they have now.

Spittle and Spines: the Curious Overcoat of the Hedgehog

THE HEDGEHOG IS undeniably one of the garden's more familiar characters. Yet its popular persona masks some surprising truths. As it shuffles around the garden with its detached demeanour – as though perpetually humming to itself – we are hard pressed to recognise this creature as the ruthless predator it really is. We might find its peculiar appearance rather appealing, amusing even, with its extraordinary spiny overcoat, button nose and small eyes. But the many small creatures for whom its footfalls are death-knells, including slugs, worms and even mice, conspicuously fail to see the funny side. And while the hedgehog may strike us as a sort of clumsy evolutionary misfit that unfortunately comes off worse when crossing roads, it has actually evolved an impressive battery of survival skills, not least the ability both to climb and swim well, and has adapted better than many species to the artificial world created by humans.

We would not, it is fair to say, really notice hedgehogs were it not for their extraordinary spines, which both defend them and define them. Without these ultra-modified hairs, hedgehogs would just look like large shrews, their closest garden relatives. Each adult hedgehog has about 5,000 spines on its body, which are constantly replenished by a continuous moult. You might imagine that these spines are exhaustingly heavy to carry around, like a very heavy fur coat, but they are actually surprisingly light, each one being hollow inside and strengthened by internal struts.

Although a hedgehog's spines are built for defence rather than attack, there is no doubt that they are impressive weapons. Each one is exceedingly sharp, and the animal has control over them, erecting them when needs be to present an array of bristling blades. In extreme danger, of course, the hedgehog curls up its body to protect its soft belly, thus ensuring that any attack would be at best uncomfortable and at worst painful to its assailant. The spines can, and do, cause serious damage: lions in Africa have been deterred by prickly hedgehogs, and few garden predators – with the notable exception of badgers – will risk attacking one.

Interestingly, the hedgehog's armour also provides it with another form of protection: shock-absorption. The spines are embedded deep in the animal's skin, but they are not straight. Instead, just above the point of entry, they curve backwards a little. This arrangement enables the hedgehog to absorb the impact of a fall more easily, and it has even been suggested that hedgehogs sometimes drop down deliberately: they are perfectly competent climbers, but when needing to get down quickly from a tree or fence, it can be easier just to jump.

Nevertheless, these wondrous spines do have their drawbacks, of which the worst is the safe haven they provide for a range of irritating parasites. Most wild animals are host to a veritable army of ticks, mites and fleas, and hedgehogs seem to come off especially badly in this department. One unfortunate individual has been logged carrying 1,000 fleas at once – although admittedly, judging by their general lack of visible irritation, the hosts seen to be largely inured to their cargo. The spines of a hedgehog, without the density or warmth of most mammal hides, are actually something of a specialist destination for fleas. It is perhaps not surprising, therefore, that there is a special flea species called the hedgehog flea (*Archaeopsylla erinacei*), which rarely occurs on anything else.

The hedgehog does not practise much in the way of spine management, but it does have one extraordinary habit that might perhaps make a contribution to hygiene. This behaviour is known as 'self-anointing'. It is a bizarre ritual, in which the hedgehog initially foams at the mouth and may look alarmingly rabid. Any fears are allayed, however, when it contorts into a series of bizarre positions and starts to lay a pool of spittle all over its spines. It doesn't do this by licking, as might a cat: no, the hedgehog uses its tongue to toss its spittle over its back, – rather like a small windscreen wiper thrusting rain sideways. Despite its efforts, coverage tends to be patchy, resulting in a hedgehog that appears to be halfway through the cycle of a car wash.

But why does it do this? Amazingly, for such distinctive behaviour from so familiar an animal, we simply don't know. Self-anointing is undoubtedly stimulated when the animal encounters powerful odours, such as the faeces of its own or other species, and this has led to the suggestion that the application of spittle might somehow absorb this odour and help conceal the hedgehog's scent from predators. On the other hand, however, perhaps self-anointing helps strengthen the hedgehog's odour in order to counteract the alien scent. Some scientists have also suggested that the layer of smelly spittle plays some role in courtship, by sending a particular message, or that it helps in everyday, non-sexual interactions between individuals. And if the spittle is really unpleasant, another theory holds, then perhaps it serves as a form of direct chemical defence against predators. Or, finally, maybe it has some sort of insecticidal property to help deal with the legion of pests. There are many theories, but so far not one has emerged as a front runner.

Truly, the hedgehog is an extraordinary and slightly mysterious animal, and by no means the vulnerable pushover it sometimes appears to be. But perhaps there is one further evolutionary pathway it could still follow. If the spines grew much longer, harder and sharper, then perhaps every unfortunate hedgehog on the road could spike the tyres that took its life away. Then, at least for a while, there would be slightly fewer cars on the road.

A hedgehog self-anointing.

Murder in the Garden

YOU WOULD THINK that, in a world where lives pass quickly and death lurks around every corner, animals of the same species would at least try to look out for one another. Our garden creatures are competitive, to be sure, and they take no prisoners in conflicts over territory, food or mates. But cold-blooded, one-against-one murder? Surely they would baulk at that.

Unfortunately, they don't. At least not all of them.

For example, just think of the question: 'Who killed Cock Robin?' The answer, at least sometimes, is: 'another cock robin'. These highly-strung birds are notoriously vicious in spats over territory and fight quite frequently. Only rarely does one of the rivals die. But it can happen.

Usually, robins keep rivals at bay with their songs. In fact, two birds singing at one another, however sweet and melodious the sound may appear to us, are trading insults in what is effectively a slanging match. This may keep birds tense, but at least it keeps them apart: the properties of a song, such as its rate of delivery and content, serve to solve arguments painlessly and at a distance. However, when rivals are well matched, the song duel may not solve a dispute, and it is then that colours have to be flaunted. The bold orange-red breast, to us such a distinctive and agreeable feature of the

robin, is actually an inflammatory badge in robin society. If one robin shows off its breast to another, fluffing it up and angling it towards its rival, the effect is similar to a finger-up gesture. It inevitably provokes a reaction: with luck, this is the retreat of one of the combatants.

But when neither of these two warning strategies succeeds, the tension may spill over into blows. The two birds fly at each other, kicking and pecking, usually aiming at the eyes and head of their rival. Genuine fights are usually

Seeing red: two robins on the verge of combat.

resolved within seconds and sometimes, at their conclusion, one scrapper doesn't get up. It is shockingly unpleasant and wasteful, like like murder of any kind.

Occasionally other species of adult bird fight each other with fatal consequences, including crows and blackbirds. The same may also happen in other strongly territorial animals, such as foxes and badgers. But it seems that, in common with robins, fights to the death are rather rare in all these species. On the whole, physical assault is a dangerous game, risking serious injury to both winner and loser.

Another well-known case of 'murder' occurs within the famously ambiguous world of spider sex. Among the garden's eight-legged creatures, females are generally very much larger than males, and we often hear tales of post-coital cannibalism – the fairer sex sucking the juices from her erstwhile partner with all the indifference of a cow chewing the cud. In reality this outcome is quite rare and the phenomenon exaggerated. It might surprise you to learn it, but most male spiders do survive copulation and live to have happy careers in repeat insemination. The most hazardous part tends to be the initial meeting (sound familiar?), when a female may mistake a suitor for potential meal.

In fact, a significant proportion of murderous incidents among garden creatures actually occurs between the young. Tadpoles are known to go into predatory mode at times and, disturbingly, they will even happily graze the corpses of adult frogs. Sometimes, however, freak tadpoles are born, which are a little larger than the others, and these routinely devour their own kind. They never grow into frogs, either, but just get bigger and bigger. Big enough, presumably, to take revenge on all those pond animals, such as great diving beetles and dragonfly larvae, that are such voracious tadpole-eaters.

Interestingly, caterpillars, which one usually associates with harmless munching on plant material, also sometimes turn cannibal – for the perfectly logical reason that there might not be much plant food available and their fellow caterpillars make good meals. The larvae of the orange-tip butterfly are notorious for this practice, as are as a number of moths.

Competition between siblings in a brood or litter can also sometimes prove destructive. The cuckoo is a famous parasite that evicts its nest bedfellows with all the ruthless contempt shown by competitors in a reality TV show. But broods comprising members of the same species also often bicker and fight with terminal results. This seems to be especially common among birds of prey, such as owls, whose sharp bills and talons are lethal weapons, even in the youngest hands.

Of all the garden murders, however, perhaps the most baffling and troubling to us are those in which adults kill defenceless babies. Once thought freakish, infanticide is now known to be widespread among animals, with plenty of examples in your back garden. One of its causes is distress: hedgehogs that are disturbed in their nests with very young cubs sometimes eat them, and both rats and mice will do the same. Sometimes it arises from oppressively high population levels, in which any further young would be unsustainable. The mother, who is the perpetrator, may judge that the young have no chance of survival, so she consumes them in order to preserve precious resources.

Another frequent cause of infanticide is one male's destruction of another male's brood or litter in order to instigate a new breeding attempt of his own. This happens in rats or mice when a new male enters a breeding arena: by killing off another male's newborn progeny, he eliminates what would to him be time wasted on childcare for someone else. At the same time he induces early oestrus in the female, hastening the potential transfer of his own genetic material.

It's not fair and it's not pretty. But then, it's murder. What did you expect?

Once courting spiders become this intimate, there is little chance of the larger female eating the male.

Brief Lives

PITY THE POOR mayfly, an inhabitant of some gardens beside rivers or ponds. Imagine being famous for the shortness of your life, and even having this enshrined in your scientific name: Ephemeroptera – which means, roughly translated, 'around for a day'. It's hardly enough to see the world, is it? Just about time for a quick tour of a garden.

A mayfly, however, might argue that at least its one day is spent profitably. As soon as they hatch, mayfly males quickly gather in swarms that dance above the water surface in poorly lit corners of ponds or rivers. They have large eyes with acute low-light vision and can soon spot an approaching female. Males have longer legs than females, and they use these to grab their welcome visitors and mate. Then, their purpose served, they die. In fact, even the term 'Ephemeroptera' may be overdoing it, since some males' lives last for little more than an hour or two of cavorting. The females, meanwhile, live somewhat longer, hanging around to deposit their eggs on the water surface, which may take a day or two.

It is tempting to think that the mayfly is exceptional in the brevity of its flirtation with

Dancing to the music of time: these mayflies may live only as long as it takes to read this book a couple of times.

This is a healthy number of survivors in a blackbird brood, though probably only one will make it to adulthood.

life. However, this same truncated lifespan is also the lot of some male aphids. Males are already alarmingly peripheral in the female-dominated world of these populous but unpopular bugs, and their appearance for a few hours on autumn days rather serves to emphasise this. The moment they hatch they are similarly on the lookout for the sexual versions of the females, and once again expire once they have mated, usually with several. The resulting eggs will hopefully give rise to a successful founder of a new colony (a foundatrix) in the spring, whereupon the population remains entirely female until male genes are required for overwintering eggs.

In fact, brief lives are the norm for many insects. Most of our butterflies and moths, for example, only live for a few days. In some species the adults don't bother to feed at all, putting all their energies into reproduction; naturally this puts a limit on their lifespan. Dragonflies may terrorise the skies above ponds and streams for a week or two in the summer with their predatory ways, but their kingdom is as short-lived as their prey. An insect's life is targeted and purposeful: time is relatively immaterial.

There are, however, some invertebrates that live conspicuously longer. There are good examples among the royal lines of social ants, bees and wasps. Although worker honeybees only have a lifespan of about six weeks, their elder sister, the queen, will span the seasons and might even live for three to five years. Queen ants, too, can overwinter, while bumblebee and wasp queens will at least last the season, although not beyond, recording a lifespan of five or six months between the early spring and late summer. Among non-social insects, some snails and slugs can live up to five years, and earthworms – which cannot breed until they are at least two years old – often last a decade. Indeed, some garden worms outlive the occupancy of those human tenants with itchy feet.

Among larger garden creatures the longevity figures become more complicated, since their projected life spans change with age. For example, only one in six blackbird fledglings tends to reach its first birthday, while the figure for hedgehogs is about one in five. However, once either of these creatures escapes the high mortality of early life, its prospects improve. Both can expect to live at least another year or two.

If we take maximum adult life expectancy as a measure, there is some fascinating variation between groups. Shrews, for instance, are fast-living creatures with a life span that just about stretches to 18 months. Toads, meanwhile, which are at least of comparable size, may live for a decade in the wild and have reached twenty years in captivity (which cannot have been riveting – if you'll pardon the pun). The main difference between the two is their respective metabolism: toads are cold-blooded and may spend months on end in a torpid state, while shrews are warm blooded and never hibernate.

It has been said that every species of mammal, no matter its size, manages to finish its life having used up roughly the same number of heartbeats. That ensures that human beings, with our fairly steady rate of 70 per minute, live a whole lot longer than shrews. The resting rate of the latter is only 88 beats a minute, but in situations of alarm or excitement it can shoot up to an astonishing 1,320 beats in one single frantic burst.

But, of course, I have actually been telling you fibs about mayflies. It is certainly true that the males only live a day, but this refers only to their adult stage and takes no account of the earlier stages: as an egg, a nymph and even a sub-adult. In fact, eggs may last the winter and it is common for mayflies to remain in the nymphal stage for as much as a year. Many other short-lived adult insects, such as butterflies and dragonflies, are also merely the tail-ends of longer journeys.

So, in this sense, the male mayfly's life span – from egg to adult – may be as much as two years. You can stop feeling sorry for it now.

The wisdom of old age confronts the energy of youth: toads can expect to live ten times longer than shrews.

JUNE IS THE month of high summer – and of high drama. For many garden creatures it is the time of reckoning. For parents the month will determine whether or not all the hassle and danger involved in reproducing has paid off. Their investments, youngsters of all kinds, are everywhere, going about their business wide-eyed and unsteady. Survival is now down to them, and many perils lie in the way.

JUNE

The Perils of Youth

YOU MAY BE shocked to hear it, but there are occasions in June when even the most dedicated gardener, on a fine, sunny, Sunday morning, neglects to mow the lawn. Those whose palms begin to sweat at the mere thought of such dereliction of duty will understand that the circumstances must be exceptional. Indeed they are – and you may even be familiar with the scenario. You step out with flex in hand and notice, on the lawn, a little, moist wriggling body. A closer look reveals that it's a froglet. Your eyes are drawn to another nearby, and within seconds you begin to see them everywhere. Soon you realise that your hallowed turf is simply crawling with them, all hopping somewhere, but not all the same way.

Every summer this same event takes place – usually in gardens with ponds, but not necessarily. It is part of the amphibian shift from water to land, something undertaken by toads and newts as well. The spawn was laid in March, the tadpoles hatched in April and now, after a risky aquatic apprenticeship in the terrors of life, the froglets spew from the pond in search of the safe havens under rocks and in the long grass that will henceforth be home. It is an epic event: an explosion of amphibian ambition, whose diminutive emissaries are hopping in random directions and against the odds.

This emergence is extraordinary, not least because it is completely unsupervised. Where, you might ask, are the parents? The answer is that they are elsewhere, safer than their progeny and inured to the fate of the year's hatching. They don't help or guide; they aren't even spectators. They would not recognise their youngsters if they hopped past and asked for directions. Of all the babies hatching out in June, the froglets are among the most completely abandoned. It seems to be the most feckless model of parenting

that you could imagine; yet it is the frogs' way, and they would no doubt claim that the abundance of productive adults is vindication of the massacres of youth.

And massacred the froglets are, if indeed they even make it to the lawn. For a start, in what is a perverse design flaw for a semi-aquatic vertebrate, young frogs cannot swim. They are, therefore, unable to hide in the water when their predators come flocking, so instead they hop and crawl around feebly by the pond-side, lambs to the slaughter. Dozens of garden animals eat them: hedgehogs, rats, owls, foxes, herons, crows, magpies. Even apparently benign characters like blackbirds are drawn to these easy meals. Huge numbers perish.

Baby-sitting bugs

The amphibian parenting model certainly appears wasteful. It isn't as though it were impossible to look after many youngsters at once, since various garden creatures manage this feat magnificently, even among the invertebrates. In some gardens there is even a bug that outperforms frogs in the parental stakes, and it has been christened the parent bug in recognition of its devotion. The female of this species lays up to 50 eggs on a birch leaf and, in contrast to so many invertebrates that simply wish their ova good luck, she guards the brood assiduously, keeping her hardened, armour-plated body over them. At the approach of danger she simply angles her body in order to shield the clutch, and should the intruder prove particularly menacing she can also flap her wings with a loud buzz and literally blow it away. Not surprisingly, the rate of successful hatching is astronomical. And that is not the end of the story: when the youngsters hatch

On the hop but not caught: young frogs leap to safety.

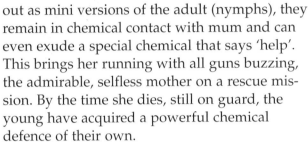

out as mini versions of the adult (nymphs), they remain in chemical contact with mum and can even exude a special chemical that says 'help'. This brings her running with all guns buzzing, the admirable, selfless mother on a rescue mission. By the time she dies, still on guard, the young have acquired a powerful chemical defence of their own.

Many spiders make no less assiduous parents. In the case of garden spiders, which are so familiar from their webs on walls, fences and rosebushes, the female lays her 1,000 or so eggs near her web and keeps guard around the cocoon until she dies in the autumn. Her vigil of a few weeks will keep most parasites at bay, although the youngsters hatch out on their own in the spring. A female wolf spider, which has no fixed web, takes parental care a few steps further by carrying the precious cocoon on her back. In this case, any predator who strikes will have to do it literally over her dead body. When the spiderlings hatch, they will have their mother around for a day or two before they disperse. After that they will, of course, be on their own, but at least this gives them some protection for those first few vulnerable hours.

There is one spider in the garden that takes parental care even further. In fact, one might fear a little for the molly-coddled youngsters when

they do finally leave the nest for the perils of the world outside. This species is known as *Theridion sisyphium*. The female looks after her cocoon carefully in the normal way and, when the spiderlings hatch, they remain *in situ*. Not only does she then look after her young and protect them against enemies: she also brings them meals. As her web fills up with prey, she sucks juices from her victims and lovingly regurgitates them to her young, one by one, mouth to mouth. One can only speculate on whether she tells them to sit up straight and not use fingers. Later, she actually takes the youngsters to the trussed up prey and pierces it, allowing them to take their turn at the extruded fluid.

Remarkable though this is as an example of devoted motherhood, you could still not claim that the young of *Theridion sisyphium* are the most cosseted in the garden. The ultimate soft start must surely be that enjoyed by the offspring of queen bees and wasps, especially those who are themselves destined to inherit the royal title. Every bee grub is born into the luxury of hive accommodation, and fed on honey and pollen by assigned workers. Most will become workers and their easy start will translate into a six-week life of hard labour. But as the summer progresses the first queens emerge. The image of pampered royalty is entirely appropriate: in common with human royalty, a veritable army of helpers and nannies attends to their every need. For young invertebrates, they are quite astonishingly safe and well fed. Many others within the colony are required to lay down their lives for these privileged, obese layabouts. And one of the first deeds of the first new queen on hatching will actually be to kill off her rivals, the as-yet unhatched grubs of similar rank. It might seem shocking but, after all, our own royal families were at this sort of thing for centuries.

As snug as a grub: bees have a gloriously indulged start to life.

Nursery duties

The idea that youngsters should be violently competitive is not an appealing one, but siblings in many of our garden animals are at each other's throats. A brood of young tits in the nest-box, for example, may be one of the more endearing images of spring, but the reality is one of violent struggle for supremacy. When an adult tit arrives with a caterpillar, it does not take a register and tick off which chick needs the next meal; it feeds to the highest bidder – the chick that is most vig-orous in its begging display. Thus the weaker individuals always get fed last, and only when their siblings are satiated (happily, it only takes one big caterpillar to fill the tummy of a nestling). The survival of the latter is therefore finely tuned to the availability of food: only when there is plenty will they get their 'share'.

Birds are, on the whole, quite devoted parents. This is partly because, for them, such care is physically possible. Birds don't go in for the mass production strategy of amphibians or inverte-brates, and thus they can devote more energy to each of their progeny. Indeed, the sheer effort they put into the welfare of their offspring can be astonishing. A good many species make hun-dreds of visits to the nest every day, bringing in the most nutritious food they can find. They are also responsible for sanitation, in the early stages taking away the youngsters' droppings – which are defecated as little sacs – in their bills. The par-ents call to the youngsters to keep quiet when a predator is near, and they refurbish the nest when it is in danger of collapsing. They even encourage youngsters to leave the nest when the time is right, and continue feeding and protecting them when they do. All in all, they are extremely effective parents, which is exactly what is required with so few youngsters to contribute to the next generation.

It doesn't matter whether you're a human being or a robin, parenting is hard work – and often messy.

June is very much a time for seeing young baby birds around. You cannot really miss them, as their juvenile feathers give them that fluffy unfinished look. They also exhibit that universal tendency of all youngsters towards locomotive incompetence, frequently flying into obstacles and making disastrous crash landings. In June they will have different plumage from their parents, too: the starlings will be mud-brown, not black; the young blackbirds will have spots, like a thrush; the tits will have yellow, not white cheeks, and the robins will have spotty upperparts and light-brown breasts.

Young mammals tend to be less obviously juvenile in appearance than the birds – though perhaps that is only because, fitted with fur, they look as though they are meant to be fluffy anyway. Mammal litters also have a much greater tendency to play than bird broods, and some of their antics offer high points in our year's wildlife viewing. The first batch of young squirrels left the drey in May, but not before treating us to scrambling chases, unintentional crashes to the ground and embarrassing moments of acrobatic mishap. This month we might be treated to the sight of fox or badger cubs playing. They fight, they barge, they mock-hunt, they leap into the air after nothing, and they generally make life extremely difficult and dangerous for any small creature that passes by – be it snail or butterfly – by sniffing, pawing and biting. Fox cubs, like their juvenile human counterparts, can also be extraordinarily messy. Outside the earth they leave a shambolic pile of playthings, from bits of rubbish to feathers, fur, bones and other remains of prey, reminding us that the carefree evenings of play are merely rehearsals for the earnest business of catching and killing that lies ahead.

And indeed, in this vein, some diligent parents of birds and mammals actually give their youngsters tutorials. Vixens and sow badgers take evening excursions around the territory with their cubs, and show off some hunting skills along the way. The same applies to parent owls: it will be weeks before the young have learned to make their own way, so for now they serve an apprenticeship in hunting. Having invested so much care in the young thus far, these very best of parents are not about to abandon the job in the critical last moments before their progeny finally take wing.

Fox cubs at play: the skills they learn in early fighting will soon be put to serious use.

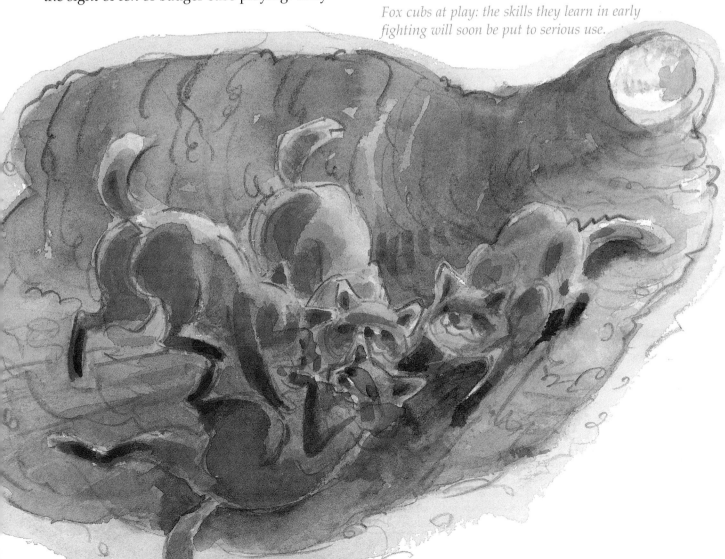

The Magic of Moths

MOTHS ARE AMONG the garden's best-kept secrets: the fortune stashed under your bed that you never knew about. If you are reading this in June, be prepared for an amazing fact: tonight more species of moths may pass through your garden than all the types of butterflies in Britain put together. Many more, in fact, because on a good night there may be over a hundred. And these will include white ones, green ones, red ones, even pink ones – moths that would really make you sit up and take notice, if only you bothered to look.

Yet moths have a bad press. Most people think they are dull and that they eat clothes. Well, some do eat clothes, but the proportion of species (two in 2,500) is so minuscule that, if were you to follow that logic, you might as well write off the whole human race because some individuals eat honey-and-baked-bean sandwiches. And, as for being dull, again it is a matter of degree. And taste. Some moths are indeed a bit brown and boring, but others are intricate flying mosaics, stunning to the eye and quite miraculous under a magnifying glass. So why are they still so unpopular? Must be a conspiracy.

Curiously, though, it sometimes seems as though that the moth community fuels this conspiracy by keeping its more spectacular members under wraps. For example, has a brilliantly colourful or outrageously shaped moth ever entered your house and flown around your lights? No. So there you are: point proven. Instead it seems that your domestic visitors are almost always the brown, irredeemably dull ones that make even the most enthusiastic lepidopterists yawn.

Maybe these have been sent by the rest on an errand to keep the moth miracle quiet.

Yet on just about every night of the year objects of wonder and beauty are indeed flying around your garden. To prove this, you have to make a bit of an effort and find them. The simplest way is to go out with a torch and a child's net at dusk, wander around the lawn next to the flowerbeds and see if you can ensnare any that cross your beam. In this way, you can entertain your neighbours as well as yourself. Of course you will be ridiculed at first, but it is remarkable how quickly your friends will be won over by the sheer wonder and diversity of moths.

One of the most striking aspects of moths is, paradoxically, their intricate camouflage. Of course, being primarily nocturnal, moths need to hide away safely during the day, so their wings reproduce the colours and patterns of vegetation in all its forms. Some resemble bark, others are green and can rest on leaves, while a few look exactly like bird droppings in an effort not to end up in the same. Not surprisingly, as the year turns and the leaves follow suit, many autumnal moths adopt glorious hues of orange and yellow. Some even mimic twigs, and always rest in a twig-like manner – even while perched incongruously on your hand. Many use curious wing shapes to break up the telltale contours of their body outline, a strategy known as disruptive camouflage, or they have large speckles and dots that do a similar job. And if their concealment strategy fails and they are discovered, many suddenly flash bright colouration or eye-spots on their hind wings at their enemies: this works like a shocking image in a horror movie, causing a momentary flinch that allows the moth a split-second chance to flee for its life.

By the time you have a couple of torch-and-net sessions under your belt, you will probably have caught a dozen or so different sorts. If by then you are inspired enough, you might wish to employ a quite different and more professional moth-catching method. Everybody knows that moths come to light, and you can use this quirk

Shock treatment: an eyed hawk moth flashes its hidden colours.

to bring them to you. All you need is a bedside lamp (with at least a 100w bulb) minus its shade, and an old sheet. Place the sheet on the lawn or patio, and simply put the lamp down in the middle of it, preferably surrounded by a few egg-boxes upon which the moths can rest. At dusk, switch on the lamp and, after a while, you will find the moths coming towards you, often in irregular circles. Eventually they will rest upon the sheet, whereupon you can examine them. Choose a still, sticky night for a moth-attracting adventure. Moths love these conditions more than any other (they are often most abundant when it is thundery), and your session could be quite spectacular. After an hour or two you will have quite a good idea of how many species are visiting your garden.

At first you will be lost in simple admiration, but soon, inevitably, you will want to find out what species you are actually hosting. And here another delight awaits: the amazing names that moths have been given. True Lovers' Knot, Maiden's Blush, Rosy Footman, Peach Blossom and Hebrew Character are all common in my garden, and you might have visits from such dignitaries as a Cosmopolitan or a Nonconformist. Any gardener with a sense of style would surely welcome a Brussels Lace, a Pine Beauty, a Clouded Border or a Royal Mantle onto their premises. A Turnip may turn up and you could have tea with an Early Grey. And it is perfectly possible for you to get three Old Ladies stuck in your lavatory – if it is an outdoor one. These marvellous names add a touch of whimsy, and perhaps a frisson of the exotic, to even the smallest of gardens.

British moths, in fact, can lay a fair claim to having the most vivid and imaginative names of any group of animals worldwide. You can just imagine these epithets being dreamed up by a group of Georgian eccentrics with too much time on their hands. "I say, chaps," one might have slurred through the haze of alcohol and tobacco, "how about calling it 'the Uncertain', because we aren't quite sure what it is?" In fact, that is pretty much exactly what happened.

Animals wouldn't acquire names like that if they weren't at least intriguing, though. Nobody got beyond the scientific names for flies and bugs, and these groups remain hopelessly underappreciated today. But moths stirred the eccentrics to raptures and they stir people still.

That's the final surprise about moths. If you start to become interested in them you will soon find that you are not alone. Did you know that there is a 'National Moth Night' every year, and a new campaign called 'Moths Matter'? All around the country, lights are going on as the lights go out.

The conspiracy will soon be over.

In the Night Garden

ON THESE MIDSUMMER nights, you don't have to dream. Instead, as dusk falls and beyond, go out into the garden. On a still evening, the reality can be just as magical.

If you start early, you can watch the swifts go to sleep. These sickle-winged birds, whose only requirement by day is still air with lots of insects wafting through it, are here between May and August, when they are a common sight over every garden – even in the heart of cities. Spending all day aloft, some retire not to an earthbound roost but to some zone of cool air about 1,000–2,000m above the ground, where they alternate long glides with occasional flaps

and take power-naps until dawn. As the sky darkens, their distinctive black shapes rise up and up, their screams becoming ever fainter, until they disappear from view into the height and light.

On most June nights daytime birds stay out late. The blackbird and robin, using their comparatively large eyes to help them to see in the gloaming, sing their last songs even when they are no more than fading silhouettes. If you are very lucky, their voices may be joined and replaced by those of tawny owls. You won't hear many hoots, but at this time of year the young are calling, with a sound very slightly like water slurping down a plughole. Their insistent pleading punctuates the peaceful atmosphere.

Bats, too, should be plying the skies about now. Dusk is rush hour for bats, because it is one of the best times of the entire night for insects. In fact, insect flight times follow precise patterns: many species fly only at twilight and rest when it is truly dark. Others take shifts throughout the night, prompted by fluctuations in temperature and moisture. The bats follow the insects' lead, alternating bouts of frenetic hunting with periods of upside-down rest. At times you can hear their clicking squeaks as they rain down sonar blips upon their flying quarry.

Your eyes might also be drawn, if you are in reflective mood, to the dances of the gnats above your head or in other corners of the garden, or even to the treetops, where swarms of tiny flies can form smoke-like plumes at this time of year, buffeted by breezes too gentle for us to feel. Most of these flies will be non-biting species and they are an underappreciated part of the garden scene, their image tarnished by their blood-sucking relatives. Why not watch them, just for a while? See how they dance individually up and down, but keep together as swarms, as though each member were attached to the rest by an elastic thread. Marvel at their energy, too: they whirl around like young people filling a club at term's end.

Soon it will be too dark to see, but don't give up on the night garden yet. This is a perfect

A swift squadron heads for the cool night air.

opportunity to use your non-visual senses. Many of the garden's blooms enrich the night air, building up bonfires of scent, such as heavenly honeysuckle. Most are primed to attract moths in a secret pact of pollination. Try listening, too. You might only hear a cat, or a party down the street, or distant traffic. But, if you are lucky, you might also just pick up a snuffle from a hedgehog.

Soon you'll need a torch. But persist. The night sees a transformation in some familiar faces. The snails and slugs are out in force, gliding around on their slides of mucus. They are more awake, alive and glistening than they ever seem by day; indeed, they appear to be gliding along effortlessly. At full tilt, they are almost elegant.

A visit to a pond at night is a must, of course. Ponds are so active in darkness that it is like visiting an all-night café. There will be numerous plops as the frogs leap from the torchlight, but you might also catch a few wide eyes on the surface. Take a closer look and you might just see

newts, too, peering at you impassively from just below the surface. Pond snails, water boatmen and pond-skaters are all active after dark.

You probably won't see many mammals, unless you live in a rural area and find yourself spooking rabbits. However, there is always a chance that your beam will reflect the eyes of a fox, which will peer back at you with a slightly yellow glow. This eye-shine is caused by light bouncing off a sort of mirror at the back of the retina known as a tapetum, the idea being that light is thus detected twice by the photoreceptor cells – once on the way in and once on the way out – and this increases the fox's light sensitivity. Cats' eyes, burning bright, have the same arrangement. However, facinating though this eye-shine is, remember that you are effectively dazzling a wild animal when detecting it, so make sure you don't watch for long.

Interestingly, the eyes of the fox or cat are not the only ones to shine in the dark, and they are not the only ones with a tapetum. The eyes of spiders are similarly endowed. If you aim your torch beam among the bushes or along fences, the sorts of places where spiders lurk, you might spot their faint glow. It takes a little practice, but after a while you will find a spider, and then another and then another.

And, for Arachnaphobes at least, that is the cue to go back inside.

Spiders' eyes shine whitish in torchlight.

Ups and Downs in the Bat Nursery

THERE'S NO DOUBT about it, bats do things differently. Small mammals they might be, but they seem to have rather little in common with conventional mammals such as mice or rabbits or badgers – except perhaps fur. For a start, of course, they can fly. And they hang upside down to feel comfortable, which is also pretty weird. And as for breeding – well, as you might expect, bats are as unusual in this aspect of their life as they are in everything else.

Now is the breeding season for bats. Indeed, during the month of June most of our bat species will give birth. But it is also the season when the males and females are roosting strictly apart: there are simply no relations between the sexes except, perhaps, cordial flypasts during night-time hunting expeditions. Certainly, it is common enough for female mammals to have brief relations with males and tend the subsequent young alone, but in this case there has been no contact at all – let alone mating – since the bats shook themselves out of hibernation.

In fact, bats mate in autumn and winter, and the youngsters that emerge in midsummer are products of that period of activity. For such a small mammal, you would imagine that this adds up to an impossibly long pregnancy – way in excess of the three weeks or so expected of a comparable animal such as a mouse. But the fact is, strictly speaking, it isn't a pregnancy. Not yet. What happens is that male and female copulate, and the male sperm is then stored in the female's body, sometimes (in the noctule bat) for as long as seven months. It is only in spring, a few days after hibernation ends, that the female ovulates and can be fertilised. And only then is pregnancy set in train. Something similar occurs with badgers, but in their case the ovum is fertilised on the spot, and it is implantation that is delayed. One of the odd results of the bats' breeding system is that frisky male bats sometimes mate with females that are torpid, in a state of hibernation, and therefore quite unable to rebuff their advances. Naughty!

Pregnancy and then lactation in bats is a fraught business. These nocturnal mammals subsist on food that is highly seasonal and unpredictable in its abundance: night-flying insects. Cold and other inclement weather dramatically affects food supplies. It can even send the bats themselves into periods of torpidity, when all their bodily functions, including pregnancy, slow down to the point of just ticking over. Thus, in bats, the length of pregnancy is highly variable, sometimes longer, sometimes shorter, which is another highly unusual aspect of their biology, since most mammals' gestation periods are quite rigidly fixed. Unfortunately, the bats' food supplies sometimes fail at the lactation stage and the youngsters do not survive, despite the excellent maternal care they receive.

But, you might wonder, do bats give birth upside down or the right way up? In fact, both have been recorded. Sometimes the mothers do give birth in their natural resting position, upside down, meaning that the youngster leaves the womb upwards. At other times gravity can be useful, in which case the mother holds on to a surface with the claws of her wings and pushes. With no midwife to hand, she cradles the baby in her tail membranes until it gains a foothold on her belly and crawls towards the teats.

The male bat is not there to witness the birth. And anyway, if he were, he might not even recognise the female he has fertilised, let alone his offspring. Instead, as mentioned above, the young are born into maternity units populated by females in various states of production. These are known as nursery roosts. They can comprise several hundred females, plus a few non-breeders and immatures of either sex, and they tend to be found in warm, sheltered sites, where the prevailing heat speeds up pregnancy and keeps the young warm. Sometimes, for whatever reason, such as disturbance, a bat will decide to change roost-site and sets off with the youngster clinging tightly to her fur.

Not only are the nursing bats single mothers, but their young are also, unusually for such small mammals, almost invariably only children. Twins are occasionally born but this is highly unusual, and most youngsters benefit from having both the female's undivided attention and all of her milk. Again, there are good reasons for this: the flow of milk depends on the supply of insects outside, and this is not always reliable. It could be courting disaster for any bat to try to raise a litter of more than one.

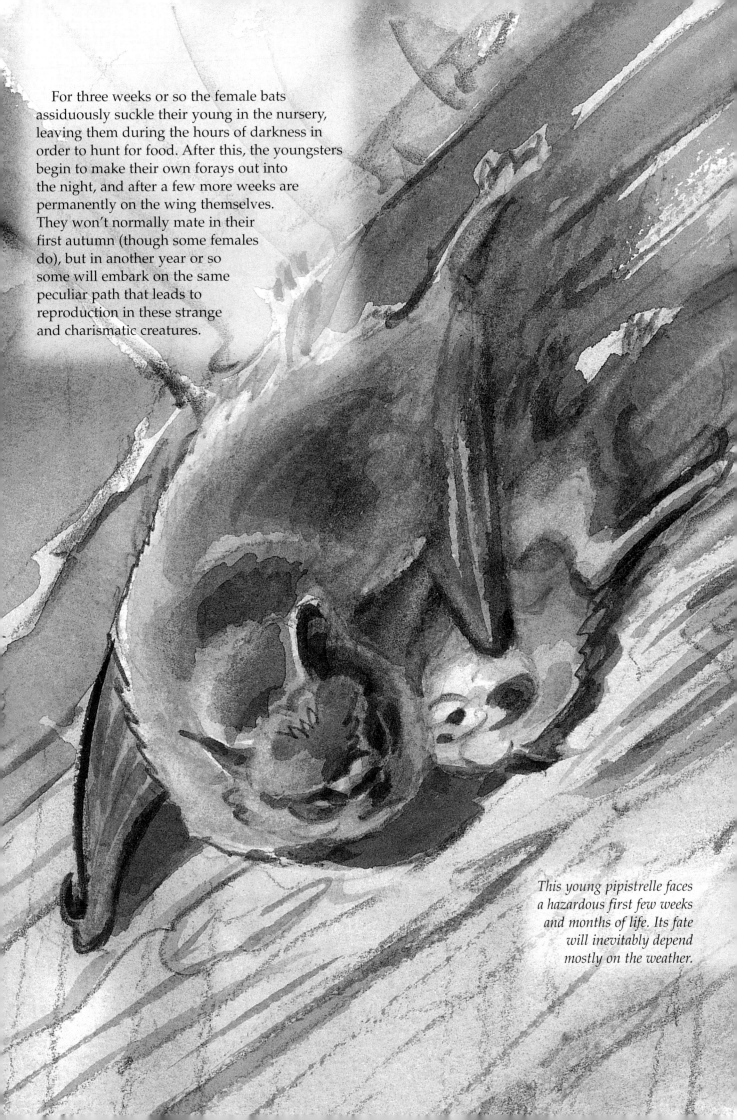

For three weeks or so the female bats assiduously suckle their young in the nursery, leaving them during the hours of darkness in order to hunt for food. After this, the youngsters begin to make their own forays out into the night, and after a few more weeks are permanently on the wing themselves. They won't normally mate in their first autumn (though some females do), but in another year or so some will embark on the same peculiar path that leads to reproduction in these strange and charismatic creatures.

This young pipistrelle faces a hazardous first few weeks and months of life. Its fate will inevitably depend mostly on the weather.

ON A GLORIOUS day in July,
with the flowers in bloom and the
newly fledged broods out and about,
your back garden can seem like the
safest place on earth. Yet behind the
scenes the struggle for life continues
as normal. Few animals can feel
entirely safe from danger – and no
animal ever too far from hunger
– in this apparently benign setting.

JULY

Turf Wars

Death in the dirt: a shrew demolishes a snail.

JUST OCCASIONALLY, WHEN we hear a noise downstairs in the middle of the night, our imagination flickers to the terrifying prospect of a malevolent intruder, some deranged killer, at large in the garden. With luck we soon calm down and go back to sleep. But in many gardens, especially ones with a little rank vegetation, those fearful instincts may actually be quite right. There is a deranged killer out there. But it's down in the leaf litter.

The shrew is a furry little mammal that isn't exactly cute and cuddly – its nose is too long and its eyes too small – but at least has some of the endearing attributes of a mouse. However, if you get to look at a shrew for long enough the warning signs begin to appear: it seems just a little manic; it twitches; it crouches and scuttles and won't look you in the eye. The more you examine it, the more you wonder. And then, with sudden ferocity, it dashes outs and sinks its teeth into an unsuspecting worm. Within seconds, the scene is an orgy of gore: the worm struggles, but the shrew is stronger and simply shreds it to death, skin coming off and body fluids exploding everywhere. It is, I assure you, quite shocking.

As the shrew moves on it encounters a beetle. Again it metes out this savage destruction, with chitin flying everywhere amidst a sickening crunching of jaws. Within a few minutes there will be another victim, perhaps a spider. And so on, relentlessly. The shrew is truly the garden's bloodthirstiest monster: it simply craves flesh. In fact, if a shrew goes for more than a couple of hours without food it might starve, so by day and night the carnage continues – the perpetrator killing and eating nearly its own bodyweight every day.

And yet shrews, for all their ferocity, are not without enemies themselves – which is why these inconspicuous animals creep about under cover of grass and bushes, or along tunnels beneath the leaf litter. This is not the behaviour of an all-powerful predator, but of a fearful animal that knows its lowly place in the food chain. A shrew even has poisonous glands on its skin as a last resort against being snatched. But although this may work against some predators, including cats, it is useless against owls, for whom the foul-smelling liquid secretion seems to be nothing more than a spicy relish. Thus, the shrew, for all its micro-omnipotence, cowers when the tables are turned.

Frogs and toads are also famous for their enormous appetites and, although it isn't quite possible to bloat them to bursting point, they have been known to excrete still-alive matter they have just eaten – after giving it a tour of their alimentary tract. And if these amphibians are not quite as unsettling as shrews, it is perhaps only because they swallow their food whole rather than acting like Hannibal Lecter. There may be less blood, but the result for earthworms, snails, slugs and various insects is much the same: slaughter.

Yet frogs and toads are also constantly in danger, which is why they usually come out at night – and also, incidentally, why they can hop so impressively. Among their many predators are some that you might not suspect,

Down in one: toads don't do chewing.

such as hedgehogs and rats, along with others that you probably would, such as foxes and herons. However, the one that must bring them out in a cold sweat is surely the grass snake. This glorious, sleek reptile can go wherever frogs go, in water and out, pursuing them relentlessly until dispatching them in the final, lingering coup-de-grace of death by swallowing. A frog's best chance upon encountering one of these graceful killers is to make the hop of its life. Toads, however, have a more courageous strategy: when eyeballed by a snake they inflate their bodies with air and stand up on their arms and legs. This makes them look a little like a crinkly-skinned concrete mixer – not especially frightening, but unde-niably large. Large enough, at least, to make even an elastic-jawed grass snake think twice.

Chain reactions

Every animal in the garden is part of a food chain. Most are links rather than end points; in other words they have both natural enemies to watch out for and living prey that must watch out for them. Thus a spider can pounce on a fly, only to be pounced on by a wood mouse, which in turn may be pounced on by an owl. Even though a garden's owner may never knowingly hurt so much as a fly, plenty of its tenants most certainly would. Food chains are universal laws of life.

But not every animal in a garden food chain is a link. Some are predators who sit at the top of their chain, doing plenty of eating but with no real enemies of their own – except, perhaps, people. These include the fox and the badger, as carnivorous mammals, and the sparrowhawk, as a carnivorous bird (although it is itself an occasional victim of other, larger birds of prey). The sparrowhawk will take anything with feathers, though nothing with fur. Both fox and badger, however, have extraordinarily broad diets. Although the badger is best known for being a worm-eating machine (see page 29), it is a genuine, tooled-up carnivore that catches and kills anything from insects to rodents and even hedgehogs.

Foxes, too, will eat worms, beetles, birds and frogs – indeed, almost any living thing they can get between their jaws. But the real prize is a delicious small mammal, such as a mouse or vole. Much as all the other stuff gets them fed, you could say that the very essence of the predatory fox is in taking this tricky rodent prey. Indeed, one of the most thrilling sights of the countryside is a fox bounding up on its hind legs like a fire-coated gymnast and landing its front paws on one of these rodents: an elegant but poignant moment of grace and death.

At the bottom of each food chain, by contrast, are creatures that eat just plant material and so are not classified as predators. These animals are often abundant: they have to be or their many enemies would wipe them out fairly quickly.

However, this does not mean that they just sit around like fruit in a supermarket waiting to be eaten. Instead they use all

Vole-catching in style.

sorts of strategies for self defence themselves. Many can fly, sprint, leap or tumble away from danger. Indeed fleeing is the first instinct of palatable animals.

But running away is crisis management. It is much better, of course, to avoid the attention of your predator in the first place. Thus concealment is the simplest form of defence. In fact, almost every garden animal is camouflaged in some way: even the bold black-and-white plumage of the magpie, for example, can be

Eyes concealed, a peacock butterfly almost disappears.

And if the 'eye' is big enough, it can actually appear quite fearsome; fearsome enough, in fact, to deter an enemy completely. The gigantic eyes of the peacock butterfly are intended to be unsettling: to an unsuspecting bird foraging in the shadows their sudden appearance must be quite a shock. Some caterpillars, too, appear so bizarre as to be unnerving: the caterpillar of the elephant hawk-moth has huge false eyes and a habit of rearing up impressively. If you doubt the effectiveness of these deterrents, just imagine yourself as a small bird, living your life in constant fear of ravenous predators, and you might begin to appreciate how they work.

Daring defences

Some of the garden's more defenceless animals eschew the security of camouflage altogether and acquire bright colours that a predator cannot possibly miss. This might sound like suicide, but the trick here is that these animals have acquired the perfect recipe to avoid being eaten: they taste disgusting. Thus any enemy that attempts to eat them will not make the same mistake again. Admittedly, some individuals must be sacrificed in order for a predator to learn its lesson, but for the collective whole, this ploy does indeed provide protection. Invertebrates that deploy this defence include the cinnabar moth caterpillar, whose brightly striped 'rugby shirt' appearance advertises the fact that it feeds on a toxic plant, the ragwort, and is therefore toxic itself. Many beetles, including ladybirds, also use chemical defence, as do such eclectic groups as bugs and millipedes.

Fascinatingly, the overall protection afforded by the unpalatable brigade may also extend to those who are not strictly members of the club. An insect may be quite palatable and harmless, yet mimic the colours and forms of the toxic or dangerous and thus get out and about with impunity. Wasps and bees, for example, have more impersonators than Elvis, among them moths and many types of fly, including bee-flies and hoverflies. For the deception to work, of course, both the genuinely poisonous insects and their mimics have to occur in the same habitats and fly at the same time of year. And so they do, like bizarre little tribute bands. This type of deception is known by scientists as Batesian

difficult to see amidst the contrasting light of dappled shade. The degree of camouflage varies, but is often remarkably effective: some of our most gaudy butterflies, like the peacock or red admiral, simply disappear when they close their wings, so subtle and drab is the leaf-like patterning on the underside. Various bugs also resemble leaves or leaves, while most caterpillars are the many shades of green that dominate the chlorophyll-packed world of the mini-beast.

Another, more subtle line of camouflage is somehow to set up a decoy for a potential predator. Many butterflies, including meadow browns and gatekeepers, use false 'eyes' (technically known as ocelli) on their wings to distract attention from the vital areas of their bodies. Experiments show that birds, their main enemies, do indeed tend to attack these eyes while leaving the rest of the insect intact.

Eye contact: a peacock startles a blackbird.

Back off! The bright colours and bold markings of the cinnabar moth caterpillar warn that it is unpalatable.

Beetles are good examples of this: all have their hind wings stiffened into a hard case known as an elytra, which protects them from many predators (though it also produces a satisfying crunching sound when breached by a hedgehog). Woodlice receive similar protection from their robust plaits of chitin. Snails can hardly depend on speed to escape, but their specially stiffened shells keep out a remarkable range of predators. At the first hint of danger, they retract into them as quickly as a television viewer flees a party political broadcast. Even the terrible jaws of shrews cannot breach snail shells.

For every form of defence, however, there is a predator with the means to overcome it. Such specialists, by concentrating on pursuing just one particular prey animal, have evolved to combat any resistance it offers. There are many examples of this: cuckoos, for example, eat all those unpalatable hairy caterpillars – even the ones with nuclear stockpiles of toxic substances; a spider called *Dysdera crocata*, with quite horrifying jaws (honestly, it could give spiders a bad name), is a specialist in piercing the armour of woodlice; and the song thrush is able to break into snails by holding them in its bill and beating the shell on a hard surface.

For most animals, there is no answer to a specialist except further evolution in the great arms race of natural selection. Eventually, as the war between predator and prey rumbles on, an individual will come up with something new and for many generations one side gains the upper hand. But in time the tables will once again be turned. That is how it is and how it has always been. Our garden turf is a rich, dynamic battleground, with the clash of heavy weaponry resounding beneath our feet.

mimicry, after the famous British biologist Henry Walter Bates.

Perhaps the most unusual form of protection in the garden comes from the practice of enlisting 'minders', of which the best-known example is the mollycoddling of aphids on our rose bushes and other plants by groups of bad-tempered ants. Now aphids, of course, are about as robust as talcum powder and would struggle to repel the attacks of a geriatric flea. But they also happen, while feeding, to extrude the most delicious of liquids from their rear ends – a best-selling, sugar-rich concoction known as honeydew. Ants adore honeydew so much that they effectively farm the aphids, protecting them from harm in much the same way that a shepherd guards livestock, and thus ensure themselves a regular supply of their favourite tipple in the ant bars after work.

There is another way in which animals can protect themselves against an enemy, and that is by decking themselves out in a suit of armour.

A snail's armoured shell is no defence against a song thrush, which has learned to smash its way in.

Slugs at the End of Their Tether

LET'S FACE IT: wild sexual abandon does not immediately come to mind when you think of slugs. Crawling along in your own slime and eating mountains of plant matter seem hardly conducive to a sex life of remarkable friskiness and jaw-dropping gymnastics. And furthermore, when you, the gardener, are putting down slug pellets, you are hardly expecting to despatch a creature whose efforts in foreplay might well be at least the equal of your own.

But the truth is that one of our garden slugs, the unadorable sounding great grey slug, is simply a master in the art of love-making. What this apparently dull mollusc gets up to on damp summer nights is such an extraordinary leap in the dark, such a feat of anatomy and such a complete expression of reproductive possibility, that it seems incredible it should be the work of two humble invertebrates.

But it is. And, furthermore, it is performed by two hermaphrodites. Strictly speaking, therefore, it is not even a necessity: by having both sets of sex organs in one body, the capacity to auto-reproduce is always there. Yet, upon meeting another of its kind, the great grey slug enthusiastically bypasses this uninteresting option and treats the encounter as an opportunity to let all its juices flow – both male and female.

The action begins just as night falls on the garden, usually during the warmer months of summer. Dusk, when their moist bodies are protected from the sun, is when slugs generally emerge. At this point many a slug will set off in search of tender leaves, but the great grey is actually more of a fungus chewer and thus often slides along walls or up tree-trunks, as well as travelling along the ground. Sooner or later its journey will bring it face to face with another great grey on a similar foray. Being such slow moving creatures, of course, slugs do not meet all the time – which may partly explain why they are hermaphrodite, to make sure they are sexually compatible with whomsoever they encounter. So a meeting is a bit special, and things quickly start hotting up. A few touches of the tentacles, and the two (or is it four?) are ready to begin their remarkable courtship routine.

The main part of the courtship is chasing – if that is the right word for a slug pursuit. The enraptured playmates begin to sidle around in circles, following each others' tails and, one might imagine, indulging in the molluscan equivalent of flirtatious giggling. One will often catch up with the other and nip it affectionately every so often, presumably chivvying it on to ever faster circuits. At any rate, the two slugs may continue this chase until the courtship arena is plastered in slime. There are various theories about how long they can keep up this routine – an hour has been claimed – but great greys are usually more impatient than this.

Sooner or later one of the revellers decides that enough is enough. It abandons the repetitive circling and begins to head in another direction. If the slugs have met on the ground, this is usually upward into the branches of a bush or tree, but if the preliminaries began above ground, it will simply head for a convenient overhang on the bark. Whatever route its new friend has taken, the second slug has no hesitation in following the lead and soon catches up, finding its frisky partner breathless with exertion and lust. Now neither slug holds back, and they enter into a twirling embrace, secreting quite indecorous amounts of

rope – often eating the mucus as it goes – or it may lower itself still further to the ground.

Of all the wonders of this extraordinary and sexy courtship dance, one question cries out for an answer: why do they do it? Wouldn't it be simpler to mate on the ground, like other slugs? The answer, it seems, is that the great grey slug is quite a large and tempting morsel to predators, so its aerial routine keeps it well clear of its arch enemy, the dreaded hedgehog.

That's as may be. But meanwhile, what an agreeable way in which to pass those hot summer nights!

sticky mucus, which appears to glue them together. Their bodies interweave like two strands of a cord, and they hang from their branch with their tails while their heads dangle in the air, tentacles twitching and exploring.

All this is impressive and surprising enough. But the most remarkable part is still to come: the twirling around, you see, coils the mucus into a rope with a quite surprising tensile strength, and it is soon strong enough to hold both molluscs. Using this rope, slowly and still entwined, the two slugs descend like acrobats and may soon be hanging in the abyss a metre below the point from which they have descended.

The end of the descent marks the start of copulation. There is now a rather flagrant flaunting of the genitals, so readers of a delicate disposition might care to turn away at this point. In molluscs, somewhat hilariously, the penis is situated on the side of the head, and this organ soon swells into a large fan shape that is clearly visible below each of the writhing animals, as though both were wearing a frothy white crown. In the great grey slug the penis may be 10cm long, half the length of its owner, so mistakes are rare and soon sperm transfer is effected. Job done, the two slugs may remain in their embrace for many minutes, writhing the night away.

Quite suddenly, however, some mutual agreement prompts the slugs to whip their genitals back out of sight and once again regain their familiar shape. They elegantly disentangle, whereupon one individual climbs back up the tether while the other remains patiently *in situ*. Eventually, with its partner gone and its eggs fertilised, it will either make its own way up the

The astounding display sequence of the great grey slug. First (far left) two great grey slugs touch tentacles. Then, having become acquainted, they make for higher ground (above), before letting themselves down on a sort of trapeze wire made by the mucus from their writhing embrace (right).

Everyone Hates Wasps

HAVE YOU EVER met anyone who likes wasps? Probably not. People might be afraid of spiders, but inside even arachnophobes is often a grudging fascination for the object of their terror. Gardeners loathe greenfly, but won't notice if one lands on their sleeve. There are those who, for their own reasons, dislike foxes and squirrels, and others who cannot bear pigeons or magpies. And, of course, we all dislike ticks and mosquitoes, but despite the fact that these insects are potentially far more dangerous than wasps, we tend to tolerate them.

Yet everybody hates wasps. The very sight of one, all vivid yellow and black, immediately make us recoil. And no wonder: wasp stings really hurt. When we were children we didn't cry when a mosquito got us, but boy did we bawl at the pain of the dreaded wasp! Wasps even have a cultural impact: they reduce the pleasure of barbecues and force a few more people in front of the television set on hot sunny days. Tragically, a small number of people are severely allergic to wasp stings and end up in A&E or even worse.

Of course, the malice of wasps, at least towards people, is wildly exaggerated. And for much of the year, if truth be told, we scarcely notice them. Most wasps spend an idyllic life visiting flowers for nectar to keep them fit and healthy. They also do a useful job in the garden by collecting food for their grubs in the form of aphids, caterpillars and other garden miscreants. It is thought that the workers from a single nest in one year may be responsible for disposing of half a million other insects, thus removing much of the responsibility of the gardener. But hey, what's half a million zapped insects when you might get stung?

Most people would probably concede that the menace of wasps is at least seasonal: we don't tend to notice them until July or August. And the fact is that this wasp 'problem', if you like, is actually

You may think your child's sweet-tooth is bad, but it has nothing on a wasp.

caused by unemployment. In common with bees, social wasps are geared towards rearing grubs from eggs laid by the colony's queen. Early in the year, this task is self-perpetuating: the workers are feeding and looking after grubs that will eventually replace them. Later on, around mid-summer, this care becomes directed towards bringing up queens, which will thrive on the food provided, growing up to be strong and robust, and leave the nest to mate and, eventually, form next year's colony. The departure of the last queens occurs in late summer and, having waved their farewells and cried their tears, the workers suddenly find that they have nothing else to do. They and the original queen are on borrowed time.

One corollary of this winding down is the waning of the old queen's influence. At the height of the colony's occupancy in early summer, the society was extremely efficient and disciplined. This happened through a remarkably strong series of chemical commands from the queen. Not for nothing has she acquired her royal title: she gives orders, and her subjects obey without question. Her body exudes a special tasty substance that the workers lick from her. This chemical, which suppresses aggression, is continually spread among the colony members as they make contact with one another, thus quashing any independence of spirit and keeping the workforce busy and peaceful. (Rumour has it that some CEOs have been after the secret of this compound for years.)

With the colony's purpose fulfilled, however, the chemistry fades and the workers are let off their pheromone leash. Life becomes a bit of a free-for-all. Many workers lose their passivity and begin to fight. Riots even break out at the nest, with many casualties. And dozens of idle workers make for human barbecues and picnics feeling bullish and uninhibited. They seek anything sweet and, for us, turn occasions sour.

Riots often break out in wasp nests at the end of the season.

The misery that wasps may cause us, however, is as nothing compared to what certain species inflict on their smaller victims. There are many wasp species in the garden, and not all are the familiar, social ones. Indeed, you could quite reasonably say that many are distinctly anti-social, since not only are they largely solitary, but they are also parasites. You probably seldom notice them, since they are generally small and inconspicuous. But to their victims they are lethal.

What these solitary wasps do seems grossly unpleasant to us. First they make a small burrow in the ground, where they lay their eggs. Next they go in search of suitable living prey, with some species specialising in caterpillars, others in flies and so on. They then attack their unfortunate victim and stab it with their paralyzing sting, before carting it off, paralysed, to the nest. Here it remains in an immobilised state until the young hatch – whereupon they find, to their delight, a hefty meal of living and thus entirely fresh food right on their doorstep. Some indeed, receive more than one such offering. Needless to say they feed avidly, during which time the parasitized insect finally passes away, having

endured what must be one of the most wretched deaths imaginable.

Unedifying though this behaviour may seem, it is certainly a very efficient way to provide for your youngsters. It also contributes to the general destruction of many of those pests that gardeners love to hate. However, this useful service probably won't alter our attitudes to these fierce, fascinating and typically ruthless insects. Everyone, from gardeners to grubs, hates wasps.

This parasitic wasp has paralysed a caterpillar and will use it as living baby-food.

Morse Code Among Spiders

Spider's webs are good for strumming, as well as for catching.

LONG BEFORE WE invented the term, let alone before it became such an abiding preoccupation of ours, spiders knew all about the concept of safe sex. To us, a slip-up can light the slow fuse to a tragedy, the terrible consequence of a half-forgotten encounter. To a spider, however, safe sex is even more of a pressing need: one slip-up can land you in the jaws of a voracious predator, who drains you of your vital juices before there is any time for recrimination or regret.

The inherent problem in spider procreation is that females are usually, to be frank, a bit large. They certainly dwarf males and, with such a disparity in size, can easily make a meal of them. When things go wrong, however, it is not generally out of spite: the female has simply tucked into her partner without having realized that he is any different to a run-of-the-mill fly.

It also turns out that female arachnids are highly particular in matters of love and need a great deal of seducing before anything exciting can happen. Thus, male spiders really do need to make the right moves. The ways in which they ease the miraculous transformation in females from fearsome predator to cooing love-kitten are many and varied. Remarkably, most involve chemical signals and some kind of staccato tapping routine – a sort of spidery Morse code.

In those species of spider that live and work on horizontal sheet webs, this routine takes the form of strumming the edge of the female's web. It is easy to imagine just how dangerous this can be, since spiders of all kinds are primed to react with speed and zest to the merest tickle of a trapped insect and will come out to meet a disturbance with all guns blazing. The male spider, having been lured by the siren scent of a receptive female, cannot help his lustful urges and, with a metaphorical deep breath, he begins to pluck. Each species strums to a different rhythm: one, for example, gives a single note every thirty seconds; others use their abdomens and legs to strike the web in time, a sort of percussion section to go with the strings. The very regularity of the beat is enough to convince the female that it is intentional and not caused by the desperate struggle of captured prey. She comes eagerly, suitably entranced, and mating takes place.

In the garden spider, which builds vertical webs, the courtship routine is slightly different. The risks are the same, but in this case the male actually strings what is known as a mating thread outside the main area of the web, and only here does he strum his tune. The routine is irresistibly similar to that of a besotted Romeo strumming a guitar for his Juliet leaning over the balcony – although mistakes in the human version are not generally punished by the performer being eaten. The male spider's task is to draw the female away from the hub of the web, where she usually waits for prey, and on to the mating thread – the only site where copulation can take place. This can be an exhausting process, especially when the female is in an unresponsive mood. Time and again she may rush aggressively towards her unwelcome serenader, trying to shut him up, only for the male to retreat by letting himself down on a safety thread of silk. It is an entertaining encounter to watch, though one's sympathies are definitely with the male.

Of course, not all spiders hunt by making webs. Jumping spiders, for example, sit around in sunny places and use their sharp eyes to spot prey, upon which they make an athletic pounce before sinking in their jaws. Courtship in this case involves a very different and far less dangerous procedure, one that is more of a dance routine than a rhythmic code. Male and female meet across a crowded lawn or wall, and the action may begin even when they are still 15cm apart. The male waves any colourful or boldly patterned part of his anatomy – his abdomen, palps, front legs or whatever, according to the species – and does so in very precise movements, which correspond to the strumming routines of other spiders. Typically, if a female is impressed she will simply stand still and allow the male to approach her and mate. Some larger hunting spiders, such as wolf spiders, perform a dance that is less elaborate but also involves strumming: they beat their legs against the surface much as we might idly strum our fingers on the table – though with eight legs involved it probably sounds more impressive.

There are endless variations on the theme of spider courtship, but all seem to be equally elaborate. In a common garden species called *Meta*, for example, the male doesn't just strum, he also offers his intended a meal. If this sounds overly generous, it should be pointed out that the male, which is about the same size as the female, is actually taking the meal from his intended's own web. It is actually the arrival of a fly that stimulates the act of courtship: the female makes for the capture and begins to truss it, but then the male intervenes and begins to truss it himself – rather like one of those annoying department store reps that insists on wrapping up goods even when you want to do so yourself. Once he has control of the bundle, he strums a sexy beat on the web and offers her the 'gift', whereupon mating takes place as she consumes it. It really is a bit like buying your beloved flowers while you are both out shopping. Not much class there.

Still, at least nobody gets hurt. Except, of course, the fly.

View to a Kill

1. *Four pairs of eyes help a zebra spider spot its prey.*

3. *Anchored by a silken thread, it pounces.*

2. *Cat-like, it edges close enough for the kill.*

4. *Powerful jaws quickly subdue the fly.*

AUGUST

WHEN WE LAZE on the sunny patio on a warm August afternoon, it's easy to be lulled by the gentle buzz of flying insects. Yet this buzz is not a lazy sound: it is the thunder of heavy traffic passing along the congested lanes of the summer air. Above our heads, summer is at full tilt. August is not quite the winding-down month we might suppose.

Heavy Traffic

THOUGH WE MIGHT doze in it, the airspace of a garden in August is as busy as a bank holiday highway. From lumbering juggernaut bees to mini aphids, and from high-performance hoverflies to steady, reliable ladybirds, the insects are hard at it. A little behind the larger animals in their schedule, many are still in the midst of a busy breeding programme, and there is still much to do.

Try something extraordinary: even if you are not very fond of insects – and let's face it, that puts you firmly in the majority – why not remain in that deckchair and actually watch them flying around for a minute or two? It is probably the easiest wildlife watching you will ever do, and you'll probably see more species of insect in a minute than you will mammals in a year.

You'll soon find that these mini-beasts exhibit an impressive range of size, colour and style. Among the most captivating of the August insect brigade are hoverflies. You seldom notice them on the flowers where they spend much of their time drinking nectar, but when aloft their speed and control is little short of awe-inspiring. And not for nothing are they called hoverflies: they can hold their position in the air as if glued there, wings pulsating at more than 300 beats per second and rendered quite invisible by their speed. Males are territorial and will chase away other members of the same species that stray into their precious one or two square metres of

private air. Females, of course, they treat quite differently, often dancing up and down in front of them and trying out different flight techniques to make titillating changes to the humming of their wings. Copulation usually takes place aloft.

Not everyone flies with quite the same expertise. Butterflies, for instance, are definitely not in the same league: they fly at a mere ten or so wing beats per second and with a distinctly unsteady look, as though a little inebriated on nectar. Butterflies have two pairs of wings, unlike the single pair of a hoverfly. These tend to be hitched together with bristles on the trailing edge of the forewing, a unique arrangement for any insect, with the two in combination acting as a single aerofoil. With their wide surface area, butterfly wings are good for long periods of flight using up modest amounts of energy. While a hoverfly needs to spend an entire morning charging up for its afternoon's territorial duties, the butterflies need far less fuel.

Insect fan or not, the chances are that you will have heard the old chestnut about how a bumblebee, aerodynamically speaking, should be incapable of flight. Of course this is nonsense: you see them buzzing about, not at all fazed. Their life is given over to collecting pollen and nectar, so imagine what hard work that would be if they had to walk. Intriguingly, the myth of the impossible bumblebee was spawned by some scientists writing aerodynamic calculations on a napkin at a dinner party in 1934 – and even at the time they were wrong, having failed to take the flexibility of the wing into account. The wine, though, must have been excellent.

Nevertheless, insects don't fly in the same way as birds or bats, and their feats are difficult to explain. For one thing, they beat their wings far too quickly for the flapping to be undertaken by muscles alone, as happens in vertebrates: a mosquito, for example, holds the oscillation record at an astonishing 600 beats a second. The secret is simple, though. An insect's wings are attached to the box-like thorax, the centre-most compartment of its body. When the wing muscles contract, they distort the elastic thorax walls, which automatically and instantly spring

Stag beetles are the wide-body jets of the insect world.

back, thus speeding the oscillation and accounting for the extraordinarily high figures.

The sheer industry of insects is proverbial, but the complexity and finesse of their lives is often overlooked. Take honeybees, for instance. We all know that they fly to and from their hive to collect nectar and pollen, but we forget that this isn't always a straightforward task, and that success is somewhat less serendipitous than it may appear. With potentially some 40,000 bees in a colony to scour the landscape, the efficient collection of resources is as much a matter of communication as it is scouting. When a bee returns from a successful foraging trip, it passes information about its nectar source to the colony at large and thereby prevents the next shift from wasting their time on unproductive missions.

The method of communication between worker bees is wondrously sophisticated. Essentially, when a scout returns from its trip it is able to give three key details about the source it has been tapping: how far away it is; in which direction; and whether it's any good. The first of these is described by a dance: if the source is close, within 20m of the nest, the arriving bee moves in a series of circles with frequent changes of direction. This is called the round dance. If, however, the source is more than 100m away, the open circles are replaced by various oscillating movements from side to side, more like a figure of eight. This is called the 'waggle dance' and is no doubt greeted by frowns all round. If the source is somewhere between 20m and 100m away, the message lies somewhere between a round dance and a waggle – enough for the audience to grasp what they need to know.

The position of the dancing bee relative to the vertical on the comb is the key to the position of the nectar. The direct vertical on the hive dance floor represents the current position of the sun, so any deviation from the vertical during the dance represents the angle at which a worker must fly relative to the sun in order to reach the source. Meanwhile, the quality of the food source is indicated in different ways according to the nature of the dance: in the round dance, the higher the quality, the more changes of direction there are; in the waggle dance it seems to be related to the amount of waggling and accompanying buzzing of the wings.

Herb crawling (or 'hover-dance'): a male hoverfly hangs above a flower, waiting for a female to turn up.

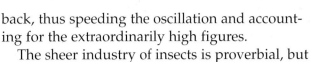

Hive and seek: in the bustle of a beehive the workers share complex information about the location of a nectar source

The sheer accuracy and complexity of these danced messages defies belief. The scout bee can even recalculate her message if she is delayed in imparting the information. The sun's position changes as bees wait their turn to dance, but the worker will know exactly how far it has gone and how long has elapsed, and when at last she gets her turn on stage she will pass on her message with all the parameters correctly updated.

Human males should note, incidentally, that these feats of spatial understanding and navigation are performed immaculately by a colony consisting entirely of females.

Late summer agendas

When you learn about the sheer artistry of the insect world, it seems almost sacrilege that these sophisticated micro-computers should ever be snapped up and squashed in the bill of a hungry bird. But talent was never a buffer to misfortune and besides, the birds of the garden need to eat. For most of them, late summer is the time to moult, a season when they need easily available resources to keep them going. It is tempting to assume that, with the end of the breeding season, August offers birds a calmer, more leisurely programme. But no, they have a pressing need to exchange their old plumage for new stock: the former is worn out, and the latter requires energy for its manufacture.

Actually, most garden birds are at their least conspicuous right now. Gardeners seeing the empty feeders and unoccupied trees often fear for the fate of their tits and robins. But the birds are still there all right, just keeping their heads down among the undergrowth, drained of their usual zest by the moult. Come the end of the month they will be back to their old selves.

In fact, some of the garden's birds and mammals are still embroiled in breeding. Nothing much halts the gravy train of small mammal production, for instance, and rodents such as wood mice could well be onto their third litter of the season, with perhaps even another still to come. August is also a time when the young squirrels of summer litters begin their exploration phase, dashing around outside the summer drey and causing palpitations, no doubt, for their mothers. A few hedgehogs will also become pregnant in August, especially if their first litter was an early one. But these late offspring will, bluntly speaking, be a bonus; sadly the individual prospects for youngsters are not good.

Down in their earths or setts, though, both foxes and badgers have finished breeding, and August is the time that their young become independent. The same applies to bats. One could forgive the parents of all these animals for taking a lie-in or basking in the sun for a while, just on those occasional August days and nights when urgency finally takes a back seat.

Among the birds, one of the habitual later garden breeders is that gorgeous, improbably plumaged sprite, the goldfinch. Highly successful individual pairs of blackbirds and robins may well still be going for the last of their multiple broods, but for goldfinches August is the height of the breeding season. The reason is simple: while the majority of garden birds feed their young on invertebrates, whose peak has passed, the main item on a goldfinch nestling menu is seeds. And seeds are everywhere in and around the garden. One of the delights of late summer is to watch these flame-winged birds, with their tricoloured heads, working the scaffolding of unsteady plant-tops as they busily extract the seeds, keeping up a steady conversation like miniature workmen on a building site.

Another set of birds you can hardly fail to notice in August is the guild of professional aeronauts: the swifts, swallows and martins. Some swallows and martins will still be engaged in breeding activity this month, but the swifts have finished, and their minds are already elsewhere as they start heading south and away from the breeding grounds. All of these birds depend on flying insects to sustain them, and a perceived slight decline in this food source – not that we would notice it ourselves– is what triggers the swift's somewhat rushed and premature departure. It is the sort of character that would put up an umbrella at the first sign of clouds in the sky.

The aforementioned insects and other tiny creatures upon which the swifts have been feeding are an interesting feature of the summer skies in their own right. Their presence, indeed, is one of the garden's great unappreciated wonders. Up above rooftop height, in a layer between about 300m and 1,500m, countless millions aphids, small flies, mites, and even web-borne caterpillars and spiders waft about the sky when the weather is fine, whisked up each day by rising convection currents and falling back to earth at night. This veritable tide of tiny bodies has been dubbed 'aeroplankton', and it is indeed the aerial equivalent of the plankton of the sea. To most of us it is invisible, but it fills the bellies of many birds, whose health and vigour is testimony to its astonishing richness.

The breeding season of the goldfinch is in full swing.

The Ants are Blowing in the Wind

THERE IS NO doubting which is the biggest day in the calendar of the black ant. This day doesn't always occur on the same date, mind you, but it usually happens sometime in August. It is a remarkable sight for you and me, and a heady afternoon's festival of sex, drugs and pizzazz for the ants. I suppose you could say it was their Glastonbury, without the music or the mud.

The day in question is the day of the nuptial flight, when suddenly winged ants break cover from our pavements, flower beds and patios and fill the air like pollen billowing from massed ranks of herbs. Normally, ants only enter our consciousness when their columns march through our living rooms in search of food, or when we inadvertently sit on their nests and suffer the consequences. But on the day of the nuptial flight – and it does usually happen on just one day a year – winged ants become a public spectacle, their multitudes buzzing past the noses of preoccupied commuters on their way home from work, forcing distressed kids inside or making a mockery of a garden barbecue. With a few bad turns they blunder into your personal space, crawling over your clothes, fluttering into your face or plopping helplessly into your wine glass. Just for a while they are uncontrollable and universal, a part of the summer air.

But if you shelve your annoyance, and remember that by tomorrow the air will have cleared, it is perfectly possible to wonder at the spectacle of nuptial flight day. The phenomenon is remarkable not just for the sheer number of small bodies involved, but also for its pivotal importance to these familiar, yet usually unobtrusive, creatures. Just as you can identify with the nerves of a bride on her big day, regardless of whether you know her or even speak the same language, so with a little imagination you can at least appreciate the energy and commitment of the ants on theirs.

Look closer at that crack in the pavement and it won't take you long to work out that there are three main character in the drama. First, there are large winged ants, which look rather like plain, dark wasps but happily cannot sting you. Second, there are equal numbers of small winged ants. And third, there are lots of ants with no wings at all, which will be running about in all directions, their excitement almost tangible. Each group has an important role to play.

The key to the drama is that both sets of winged ants are about to embark upon the only flight of their lives, and during their time aloft they will also be seeking to mate for the only time in their lives. The big flying ants are females, all potential future queens. The smaller flying ants are males, potential suitors for queens from different colonies. The two sexes will mingle in that great cattle market in the sky, where ants from all the neighbourhood colonies swarm and copulate.

The other players in the drama are the sterile workers, whose job it is to prepare the sexuals – as the winged individuals are known – for their flight. Their role has been a lengthy one: they have nurtured these protégées from the grub stage, brought them close to the surface when the time drew near, and have been responsible for getting the day right. Today they fuss about like mothers of the bride, running up and down, attending to the needs of everyone, utterly engaged in the business of the day. With just a little imagination, you can picture them straightening the ties of the males and the hems of the

Ants fly only once in their lives, but they do it with style.

females. You half-expect them to shed a small tear at the moment their charges take flight.

And take flight the sexuals do, always into air that is humid and still. That is how the colonies manage to co-ordinate their emergences: they respond to exactly the same atmospheric conditions and state of daylight. Black ants come out in the afternoon, while for other species it is the morning or even daybreak. Ideally, for the black ants, there will have been a downpour of recent rain, followed by a period of warm, settled weather. It is also likely that the first ants to emerge send chemical signals into the atmosphere, soon luring the more bashful colonies into action.

Once airborne, the individual ants are completely single-minded. They take no precautions, and thousands are guzzled by gleeful birds, which themselves exhibit great excitement at the nuptial flights, flying around like kids set loose in a sweetshop. Swifts, swallows and house martins, being professional aerial insect catchers, take the most victims, but many local opportunists also join in, including house sparrows, starlings and even black-headed gulls. The carnage is incalculable.

Enough males invariably survive, however, to form mid-air swarms to which the remaining females are attracted. Almost as soon as the latter arrive, each is grabbed by a suitor and, because the females are so much larger than the males, the couple remains aloft while mating takes place. In the maelstrom of the afternoon's activity, at least some individuals of either sex are thought to copulate more than once if the fancy takes them. But after this day, neither will do so ever again.

Indeed, a male's time in the world will soon be at an end, for the nuptial flight is both the high point and the culmination of his life. Within hours, every male in the swarm will be dead.

The females, meanwhile, are now destined to be the future queens of a colony – that's if they survive the flight down to earth and can find a suitable spot to set one up. This is no simple matter and some females, having beaten the odds and made it this far, stumble into existing colonies and are immediately despatched by the incumbents. Others, however, manage to find an inviting crack in a wall or burrow into some suitable earth, where they will eventually reproduce, using their recently acquired sperm to propagate many thousands of progeny, and spawn a colony single-handedly.

First, though, they must deal with their wings. One might expect these to wither away gradually. But no, the female breaks them firmly off and draws a line under her former life. The business of working new ground can now, at last, begin.

Worker ants fuss over their queen's grubs with almost maternal passion.

Tit for Tat in the Night Sky

WHEN DUSK FALLS over many of our gardens, bats come out and harvest the insect traffic of the darkening summer skies. Gardens, indeed, are ideal for bats, providing little zones of plant diversity that breed plentiful flying meals and shoot them into the sheltered air between four walls or hedges, where foraging is easy. And the bats take full advantage: they are voracious predators, and a pipistrelle, for example, may eat over 1,000 midges in a night. Were it not for bats, just imagine how the night air might seethe with unfettered life. The midges, moths and beetles would have free rein to swarm unchecked all over our airspace.

At first sight the plunder that the bats take above our heads would appear to be one of life's uneven battles. Bats are ultra-sophisticated killing machines, fitted with bio-sonar to home in on unseen targets. Their prey items are mere insects, bless them, creatures that are mass-produced and fitted with simple components at the cheap end of the market. What chance do they stand?

A bat's technology is called echolocation: pulses of high-frequency sound waves produced by the nose or mouth are sent forwards to bounce off hard objects and return with information, like echoes. Thus, once a moth or another insect comes within about 5m, a blip appears on the bat's screen, so to speak, and by increasing its rate of calling the predator can then zero in on its target. Some bat echolocation systems are so efficient that they can even distinguish different types of moth by the way in which they flutter their wings.

Of course, moths do not go willingly. But at first sight their attempts at escape appear pitiful. Many fly in a crazy, haphazard pattern that is so unpredictable as to bamboozle even the bats' instruments. And some hide themselves away among leaves, so that the waves bouncing back are too complex and confusing for the bats to decipher. But these strategies don't always work. When a bat is sending out a volley of signals 200 to the second, as some species do, it can follow even the most confusing of pathways. The echolocation of the noctule bat, for example, is so sensitive that it can actually pick out moths sitting still on a leaf, despite their attempt at 'acoustic concealment'.

So that's game, set and match to the bats, then? Well, not quite. Some moths are pretty helpless, but not all. It so happens that among a minority of moth families there is a surprise weapon that balances things up a bit. It appears that some moths have ears.

These ears are rather primitive: some only have two or four vibration-sensitive cells connected to a minute eardrum, which is a pretty tenuous claim on a sense of hearing. Yet they are so effective, and they tune so well to the frequencies that the bats use in their echolocation, that the moths are actually able to hear the bats coming. And, better still, a moth can detect a bat at 20–40m, long before the bat is aware of it.

What is a moth to do, though, when it hears a bat coming? Flying madly about is a bit chancy. It turns out that the safest place for a juicy invertebrate to be is on the ground among the grass or leaf litter. Therefore,

Pip squeak: the pipistrelle, like other bats, uses ultrasonics to catch flying insects.

The moth drop: sometimes the ground is the safest place when bats are about.

either the moth just stops flapping its wings and lets gravity suck it to safety, or it revs up and makes a power-dive down. Either way, we garden watchers are missing what must be quite an amusing sight: dozens of moths dropping like stones, one after the other, at the approach of a bat.

Although many moths are deaf, the presence of this counter-espionage equipment would appear to tilt the moth/bat balance in favour of the insects. However, bats are unwilling to abandon any potential items on their menu, especially since some hearing moths, such as the large yellow underwing, are both abundant and mouth-wateringly chunky. So now it is the mammals' turn to fight back.

This time it's a battle of frequencies. In general, moths can only hear well in the 20–60 kHz frequency range (20 kHz is at the top of our audible range). Therefore some bats have, during this evolutionary arms race, altered the pitch of their echolocating calls so that the moths cannot hear them. Horseshoe bats, for example, tend to use hunting calls below 20kHz or above 60kHz.

Yet scientists have recently discovered that moths, in response, can use their ears to respond to the varying frequencies used by bats. The large yellow underwing seems able to follow the auditory range employed by a hunting bat as it forages and approaches. Once the moth's ears are tuned to the correct frequency, they remain alert to it for several minutes in case of a further attack. It seems that this ability, which is unique in the animal kingdom, provides an exceptionally effective barrier against bat attack.

And yet the bats still have one more auditory trick: they can whisper – just like schoolchildren who don't want to be heard. And it doesn't matter how well tuned in a human teacher might be, some whisperers will inevitably remain undetected. So when the so-called 'whispering bats', such as the brown long-eared bat, fly softly

among the foliage putting out quiet signals, many moths succumb.

But even then, some moths are immune to even the most determined of bats. These include a number of groups, such as the tiger moths, that are brazenly colourful by day and fly with brash confidence by night. Their security lies in the fact that they are unpalatable. Should a bat attempt to eat one, it would receive an unpleasant shock and a nasty aftertaste to remind it not to repeat the mistake. These moths are fully aware of their own distastefulness. But how do the bats know their targets are unpleasant to eat when they cannot see the warning colours? It's simple really: the moths tell them. Certain moths can make the same sorts of ultrasonic clicks that every bat can understand, so when a hunting bat approaches an unpalatable moth, a few clicks warn it to veer away. It would certainly seem that these moths are the winners in this particular conflict.

Moths, like this red underwing, are not sitting ducks; they try to avoid being eaten by anything, including bats.

The truth is that there have to be both winners and losers – as in all predator/prey relationships. Over time, plenty of bats need to fill their bellies, while plenty of moths need to escape and reproduce. Natural selection ensures that when one constituency gains an advantage, the other soon fights back. What has surprised researchers over the years, though, is just how complex and sophisticated the moths, with their simpler anatomy, have proven to be.

There is, however, one other group of moths that has acquired almost complete immunity to bat attacks. Many thousands of years ago these moths saw the arms race coming and reverted to flying by day instead. We now call them butterflies.

Who'd Be a Vole?

IN THE UNLIKELY event that the lot of people, upon death, is to be reincarnated as another creature, I have some advice for you: don't, whatever you do, come back as a vole. Really. Just don't go there. The life of a vole is about as stressful and disagreeable as it is possible to get.

If, when watching documentaries on African wildlife, you've ever felt just a tinge of sympathy for those gazelles that all the predators seem to chase in slow motion until the director cuts to the munching of the carcass, you will appreciate the predicament of the vole – that mouse-like, shortish-tailed little mammal that might live in your garden if you have a few bushes or some rank grass. Voles, like gazelles, are harmless herbivores that happen to be very successful and abundant. They also, sadly, seem to be rather foolish creatures. Why else be active by both day and night, when everything that could eat them does so? Their list of predators is as long as a WAG's shopping list. This means that everything they do they do in a hurry – until those wicked talons or sharp teeth come calling.

Snack, anyone?

One of the vole's many enemies is the kestrel, a small bird of prey that sometimes hunts in larger gardens. Kestrels usually search for food with a characteristic hovering flight, holding a steady position over a field, flapping into the wind but keeping their head perfectly still. This technique enables them to spot the voles when the voles cannot spot them. But kestrels also have another talent that puts their prey at a huge disadvantage: they can detect the ultraviolet reflectance of vole urine. This means that kestrels can monitor the abundance of voles in a certain field or lawn just by looking over it, then search out the best places to hunt. In theory it could also mean that kestrels can catch voles in the act of spending a penny.

The terrible truth here, though, is that urine is a vital part of the voles' communication system. In common with many garden mammals, voles scent-mark their territories and use their noses to assess relationships and social status. In short, urine is extremely important to them, and they pee rather frequently. Just try saying to somebody: 'Urinate in the next hour, and you're dead!' They'll be desperate and cross-legged within minutes. So the chances of voles controlling themselves are next to nothing.

The vole's smelly status is also highly instructive for an even worse enemy, the weasel. More gardens host weasels than you might think, and these diminutive, slinky carnivores are true vole specialists – although they may also take other small mammals when they visit your precious patch. A weasel can hunt a vole by smell, and its frighteningly refined nose can read detail from the scent. For example, it can tell the age and reproductive condition of a vole, just as voles can among themselves. Thus, in a really sinister twist, a weasel can target with deadly accuracy the most vulnerable individuals in a population, those females that have just given birth. They make a delicious and easy target, and the litter they have just spawned adds the perfect relish to the meal.

This war of the noses is not completely one-sided, though, because weasels also go about spreading scent through their anal glands, and the voles can therefore work out their whereabouts. When the scent of weasels is strong in an area, the voles react by not getting out much – or they concentrate on feeding above ground, where it is safer. But there is a trade-off between being safe and being hungry, and sooner or later even the most timid vole will have to leave its burrow, or it will starve.

Remarkably, the presence of weasels can directly influence a vole's breeding programme: with the predators on the prowl, vole reproduction is suppressed because it is simply too dangerous. 80% of females suspend breeding, and those that don't tend to be older females that are on borrowed time anyway.

Well actually, in a way, every vole is on borrowed time. It has been estimated that only 70% of a given population of voles will remain alive from one month to the next, so the process of breeding, when the olfactory world is free of weasel stink, takes place with astonishing speed. In common with many small mammals, voles are geared to fast reproduction and rapid turnover: gestation in the bank vole lasts a mere 17 days if

there is plenty of food around, and female young, once born, can be sexually mature in only four weeks. The males take twice that long, but overall this still means that a given female could produce up to four litters of four young, which themselves could be in the breeding population within a few weeks. Not surprisingly, vole populations can build up very quickly indeed.

In this kind of breeding cycle, though, the impression is that individuals are almost expendable – and you may not be surprised to learn that voles belong to the same sub-family as lemmings. The very most that any vole could possibly live is about a year and a half; by then it will effectively have white hair and be walking with a stick. The brutal reality for voles is that death does not hang around.

So maybe the idea of being reincarnated as a vole is not so bad. If you only live eighteen months, at least you will be recycled at impressive speed and make a more sensible choice next time around. A giant tortoise, anyone?

Weasels take a terrible toll of the small mammal population, especially voles.

THE START OF autumn signals all sorts of changes in the garden. Some are obvious, such as the way in which tired summer greens explode into bright yellows and browns. But others happen almost invisibly. Behind the scenes, for example, there is a big changeover of personnel among birds and mammals – a profound resettlement of which we may be completely unaware.

SEPTEMBER

All Change

SOME TIME THIS month, choose a still, clear night, go out into your garden and look up at the stars. As a wildlife watcher you won't see anything and you probably won't hear anything; but that doesn't matter. It is your imagination that counts here, because up above you something special is happening, something that very few people have ever witnessed.

That air space above is no less than a bird super-highway and, in seasonal terms, September nights constitute its annual rush hour. If conditions are right, with settled weather and a gentle northerly breeze, then on any given evening migrating birds will be moving over almost every corner of northern Europe – and that includes your garden, wherever it may be. If you could rest an improbably tall ladder against your house, then climb into the darkness and wait, you would soon find yourself in the middle of a busy, three-dimensional aerial motorway, with a constant stream of small bodies fluttering past. And on this motorway there's no gridlock, the engines are quiet, and everybody travels with care and concentration.

Everyone knows that birds migrate, of course, but few realise just how close at hand the phenomenon can be – and how spectacular. Thousands of birds may pass over your house on any given night, several every minute, many flying in groups. And, perhaps most excitingly, these travellers may include many species that you would never expect to cast a shadow – albeit a moonlight shadow – on your hallowed turf: birds such as ring ouzels, whimbrels and pied flycatchers, all hailing from wild landscapes far removed from your humble garden. September nights bring them over, unseen and uncounted – indeed, uncountable. A great tide of migration washes over our unremarkable neighbourhoods, while we sleep on, oblivious.

At times, however, we can detect the aftermath. In the morning after a major migratory movement you might notice that the garden's birdlife has changed a little, perhaps revealing a more unusual bird mixing it with the familiar blue tits and greenfinches. There might be a blackcap feeding on some red berries shining in the morning dew, for instance, or perhaps a diminutive willow warbler flitting about the shrubbery. These travellers are proof of the existence of the aerial super-highway and, to them, your garden is the welcome service station under the flyover. They might stay a day or two or just a few hours, depending on their own condition and the amount of natural food your garden offers. But soon they'll be off again, en route to exotic destinations in southern Europe or Africa.

Although most of these journeys takes place in the darkness, some species do travel by day, which makes their migration easy to observe over your own home. Swallows, house martins and swifts fall into this category. In fact, most swifts will have departed for Africa during August – they are among the first migrants to leave – but on some days, especially those with a favourable northerly breeze, you can watch streams of the other two species passing overhead, wherever you are.

An exotic pied flycatcher could enliven the garden scene in September.

The admiral goes to sea: some butterflies will be on a southward journey and may end up by the shores of the Mediterranean.

You can tell that these aerial birds are on their migratory flight by the way that in which they move. There is none of the usual flying back and forth, making haphazard patterns in the sky; migrants fly just above the rooftops in parties, straight and unwavering, with no time for their usual playfulness.

Mini-migrants

Birds are not the only migrants that might make windfall in your garden in September. You will inevitably play host to some insect migrants, too, and in many ways their movements are even more remarkable than those of the birds.

The most obvious of these, although not necessarily the most numerous, are butterflies, which can arrive in your garden from all kinds of destinations, near and far. Take the red admiral: the individual feeding on the last buddleia of the year, or on the first blooms of ivy, has quite an ancestry and, potentially, quite a future. Its grandparents will probably have been north Africans who emigrated early this same year and settled somewhere in central Europe. In turn their progeny also grew itchy feet and moved north, travelling on favourable tailwinds, perhaps arriving in Britain in June to breed. Thus your individual might well have been raised

A migrant such as this willow warbler could be in your garden one day and in Africa by the end of the week.

locally a month or two back. However, with the coming colder weather, and with the mists of dawn and dusk effectively prolonging the night, it could now be joining a new movement back south again. In a few weeks this same butterfly could be supping nectar along the shores of the Mediterranean.

But not all butterflies follow such grand schemes. Some may be making more local journeys, measured in tens rather than hundreds of kilometres. A small white visiting your herbaceous border on its way south may stop at the south coast, or settle to breed within a few kilometres of your garden. Within any given butterfly species there is great variation. Indeed, individuals of some species will still be travelling north. These travellers, which include some red admirals and painted ladies, are probably heading for oblivion, since neither they, nor their eggs, can survive the first frosts of winter.

Their prowess in the air, albeit somewhat feeble-looking to us, at least gives butterflies a choice about where and when to travel. They don't need to fly when conditions are rough, and they can choose the appropriate tailwinds for their journeys. But this is not the case with every waif and stray in the garden: some simply arrive helplessly, hitched on a crazy ride with an unknown destination. Indeed, if you really want to know which is the most surprising of all the garden's foreign visitors, then take a deep breath, dive among your beans and give some grudging respect to the humble aphid.

You might remember that, in late summer, convection currents snap up minute insects and parachuting spiders and waft them high into the air to form the 'aeroplankton' layer (see page 101). Well, every summer the winds catch these clouds of insects and blow them considerable distances from their origin on a one-way ticket. Many of the bean aphids that we are so irritated to discover on our

vegetable patch, for example, are known to have originated – a generation or two back – in central France, carried on northerly and westerly winds. Some of the very individuals we find resolutely sucking our vegetables' juices will have hitched a ride across huge tracts of hostile land or sea, where any fall to earth would have proved fatal. We may not like aphids, but it is hard not to be impressed by their pioneering spirit.

Stars in their eyes

The arbitrary nature of the aphids' helpless, wind-borne migration raises the question of how more 'willing' travellers – those that migrate purposefully – move in their intended direction. We know that both birds and butterflies travel north in the spring and south (birds and a few butterflies) in the autumn, but the mechanisms by which they manage to find their way help remind us what complex and sophisticated creatures they are.

Many organisms are capable of using a number of cues, of which the most obvious is the sun. As we know, the sun moves predictably across the sky each day, enabling even us – desensitised as we might be by modern living – to orientate ourselves in a particular direction if need be, especially if we know the time of day. But both birds and butterflies are sensitive not only to the sun, but also to polarised light, allowing them to detect the location of the sun even on the cloudiest days. Thus both these winged travellers can use our star to lock on to a particular direction of travel. Birds also have efficient body clocks, so they can adjust their bearings according to the time of day. Butterflies don't, so when flying south they simply keep the sun ahead of them; in the morning they begin by flying southeast, but gradually switch to southwest by the afternoon.

By dusk, as we have seen, many birds are preparing for their migratory night flight. Typically they leave early, when the polarised light pattern still gives away the last position of the sun, but as the night progresses they have to rely instead on other celestial clues – the stars. It has been shown that birds don't carry a specific map in their brains, but instead follow the movement of constellations around the Pole Star, which in our hemisphere tells them the direction of north.

Remarkably, there is also strong experimental

Moonbeam migrants: many thousands of moths arrive on our shores in September after a long sea crossing.

evidence that moths can orientate themselves by the stars in the same way as birds. One of our commonest autumnal species, the large yellow underwing, which often migrates here in large numbers from the continent, has been shown in the laboratory to follow artificial movements of constellations. Interestingly, unlike birds, this moth will also use the moon for orientation, keeping itself slavishly at a certain angle to our satellite regardless of the latter's progression across the sky. The flight path is far from straight, but the overall direction is consistent. Incidentally, moths' propensity for moon-orientation might be at least partly responsible for their curious attraction to light sources – although our light bulbs make a very meagre and unsatisfactory substitute.

Finally, migrating birds, moths and butterflies also have some sensitivity to the earth's magnetic field; indeed, in birds this may be the single most important of their migratory senses, and it is now thought possible that they can 'see' it through special receptors in their eyes. This ability makes it relatively easy to orientate north to south, although the precise mechanisms by which animals interpret magnetic cues are still unknown.

On their own four feet

While gasping in amazement at the migratory feats of our aerial garden migrants, we must not

overlook the fact that more mundane, though no less significant, movements are also going on down below, where feet rather than wings are the agents of propulsion. While some of these garden creatures may not 'migrate' in the broadly understood sense of the term, they undeniably travel. And the result, either way, is that new individuals of many familiar species may be entering the garden. There is thus yet another change of cast on the garden stage.

This type of movement is better known as dispersal, and it mostly concerns young animals in the first few months of their lives. Except among badgers, in which the year's young typically remain in their natal territory and become members of a social group, it is behoven upon young mammals – including our own species – to leave the family home when they grow up. The reason is obvious: it does not pay for a youngster to compete with its parents and siblings for territorial resources, nor indeed to remain so close that inbreeding could occur. So, when the time is right, the youngsters just walk away. One day they set off on what may seem like just another trip to find food, and do not come back.

On the whole our garden mammals don't travel very far when dispersing: a couple of kilometres usually takes them into a foreign neighbourhood where they can settle. But there are exceptions. Hedgehogs have been known to disperse 15km and foxes, remarkably, as far as 40km (in North America, an amazing 250km). Even young moles, which are excluded from the security of their natal burrow, may be obliged to travel a kilometre or more.

These journeys of dispersal, which incidentally are also undertaken by young birds of both migratory and non-migratory species, can be as unpredictable and hazardous as the treks of legendary explorers. Foxes may have to cross rivers, hedgehogs are even more susceptible to the perils of roads than usual, and moles may find themselves in that strange world of the above-ground – they have even been recorded swimming across ponds. For all species, the autumn dispersal is a time for testing and stretching all kinds of boundaries.

It takes more than a garden fence to halt a hedgehog.

Fox trot: roads are no barrier to fox dispersal.

So if you are still standing there on your crisp September night, looking up towards the busy airways in the sky, remember to look down, too, into the garden's shadows. That fox you glimpse may be no less a traveller than the birds you cannot see, itself moving on in the darkness, each footfall purposeful, risky and new.

Dad's Army

IT TAKES A lot to make a moth clattering ridiculously against a window pane or light bulb look elegant. But, somehow, there is one type of insect that manages. This particular character, indeed, could make almost any other insect appear poised by comparison. It is the daddy-longlegs, the most incompetent, gangling and plain ludicrous of all our garden insects.

September is a good time for daddy-longlegs – or a bad one, depending on your opinion of them. This is the season, at any rate, when these flying disasters are at their most abundant, and when they can so often be seen entering places they really shouldn't, such as living rooms, bedrooms and bathrooms. The problem is that they are so ridiculously abundant that, inevitably, some are attracted to lights and stray from the long, long grass of home into the less welcoming domain of the householder.

Remarkably, some people are scared of daddy-longlegs – many even mistaking these aerial creatures for spiders. The fear and the confusion no doubt lie in the fact that these insects do have extremely long legs, which seem to splay out in all directions. But daddy-longlegs are completely harmless. They are not spiders, but insects. And, like most insects, they have wings. Their lot in life is to drink plant fluids and have sex. Each individual lives for just two or three days, and if during this time it succeeds in achieving both goals, it can be judged a success.

Technically the daddy-longlegs should actually be called the crane fly. It belongs to the same group of insects, the 'typical flies' (Diptera), as those annoying, but much more efficient-looking blowflies that buzz around in kitchens and settle on food or refuse. The similarity may not be obvious at first, but both these types of fly have

Cranefly chaos – and carnage – is a September ritual.

only two wings, whereas most other insects, including bees, hoverflies and dragonflies, have four. In fact, crane flies are the largest of all our flies: one species (we have over 300) that is sometimes found in gardens can boast a wingspan of 65mm, which makes it one of our biggest insects. And yes, you could meet it on a dark night.

You can readily sex crane flies, should you want to: the tip of the abdomen is clubbed in the male and pointed in the female (for laying eggs in the ground). Females release pheromones as soon as they hatch out from their larval form, which attract amorous males from some distance to meet their leggy fancies. Once a pair meets up, they head off to the privacy of the long grass, where copulation takes place.

One of the anatomical oddities about crane flies is that their exceptionally long legs are actually surprisingly expendable. It seems that the slightest accidental touch will remove the odd segment or two, and if a crane fly really gets into a stew its limbs may begin to fall off at the sort of rate one might recollect from a Monty Python sketch. Much as we might be horrified, and wince at the thought of its suffering, it seems that the animal itself treats this loss almost with indifference. In fact it has been shown that a crane fly, having started life with six legs, can carry out all its essential tasks quite effectively even with only three.

Another interesting anatomical feature is the crane fly's wings, which, unlike its legs, are indispensable. Most flies hold their wings over their bodies at rest, but larger crane flies hold their wings out, rather like a poor man's butterfly. This enables intrigued wildlife enthusiasts to see two small projections behind the wings on the thorax, looking a bit like small car indicator rods. These are organs known as halteres; they are fitted with a battery of microscopic sensors that convey information about air currents and the stresses incurred during flight.

Once two crane flies have mated, the female makes her way down to the soil to deposit her eggs. She will lay about 300 of these, which hatch within a couple of weeks into larval delinquents. No longer is the crane fly a figure of good-humoured fun: it is now a pest hated by gardeners and farmers alike. The daddy-longlegs has tuned into its alter ego, the dreaded leatherjacket.

It is perhaps just as well that the mother crane fly never gets to see her offspring, for the leatherjacket is so ugly that it could seriously strain the

Legs and Co: this cranefly is a female.

very limits of maternal devotion. This dark, slimy creature, with its huge, lippy mouth at one end, looks rather like a terrestrial version of a seaslug, and makes a normal maggot seem almost attractive by comparison. Eventually, it might grow up to 3cm long.

And that is three centimetres of trouble. Leatherjackets, like larvae everywhere, spend much of their time eating. They live in the soil and munch underground vegetable matter such as roots, tubers and corms – including the roots of lawn grass. This career of non-stop vegetarian destruction can span up to 11 months of the year, right through the winter. The damage they cause can be serious, with grass and other plants simply dying off. On the plus side, however, they make excellent meals for a variety of ground-foraging birds, notably starlings and crows.

So it turns out that the army of ludicrous insects that crashes around your garden in the autumn, legs flying, is not quite the comic event that it might at first seem. For gardeners, it signals a very real invasion, albeit one that is deep in the soil and out of sight.

Stripes Versus Prickles

IF YOU WERE to look at a picture celebrating garden wildlife in a book published some time during the last century, you would probably find badger and hedgehog depicted feeding amicably together on the lawn, side by side. This agreeable image would indicate the potential richness of the semi-rural garden, with these two popular animals, together with the fox, as its crowning centrepiece.

These days, however, we know of a darker side to the relationship between these fellow lawn-hoovers. It seems that, far from being amicable, the connection between them is more one of predator and prey, and you would thus be highly unlikely to find them sharing your lawn in peace. Indeed, if you are particularly taken with hedgehogs, I suggest you either brace yourself for what follows or skip quickly to the next section.

Older books on badgers did note that these predators sometimes ate hedgehogs. However, the practice was held to be rare. You would read the odd report explaining how the deed might be done: it seems that, by using their long, sharp claws, badgers can get between the hedgehog spines and simply rip open its flesh – or else they unfurl the curled up creature and tear it down the belly. Either way they make a neat job of it, eating all the innards and avoiding any injury by leaving the head, spines and skin. It is easy to forget that, despite their obsession with worms, badgers are highly skilled carnivores.

In recent years, however, it has become clear that such unfortunate incidents are far from occasional, and that hedgehogs are actually in great danger whenever they encounter a badger. We now know that, in the classic mode of several predator-prey relationships, it only takes the scent of a badger to make a hedgehog's blood run cold. Hedgehogs will avoid any areas riddled with badger scent, even if the predator is not in evidence, and hedgehogs are most numerous where badgers are scarce. There is a proven correlation between populations of the two animals, with the hedgehogs coming off worse.

The last roll? This hedgehog is in serious trouble.

Yet it seems highly unlikely that badgers ever actually set out at night in search of hedgehog flesh. There simply are not enough hedgehogs around for a badger to be such a specialist predator. The unfortunate thing for the hedgehog, however, is that the two animals belong to the same feeding guild, seeking out the very same prey in the very same places – namely worms on grass. Thus they invariably come across one another in the course of their foraging. It is like somebody putting a contract killer on your tail who, by unfortunate coincidence, happens to share your workplace. Worms are a specialised foodstuff, and any worm-eater worth the name soon learns the best places to find them. Badger and hedgehog are thus thrown together.

Fortunately for the hedgehog, however, it does hold one major ecological advantage over its foe: it has found a comfortable accommodation with people and their ways. Badgers, on the other hand, have long been persecuted for one reason or another (most recently because they can be carriers of bovine tuberculosis), and are fundamentally afraid of us. True, they will enter gardens and eat dog food put out for them, but to persuade them to do this takes considerable effort, and they have never really become familiar animals in the wild. Hedgehogs, on the other hand, will wander blithely across lawns when people are still about. They can also penetrate into large urban areas, where badgers are seldom found.

It turns out that the hedgehog's ability to fit into suburbia has almost become its lifeline in the UK. Recent studies have shown that rural hedgehogs are effectively eliminated above a certain badger population density, corresponding to 0.23 main setts per square kilometre. Wherever the badger population exceeds this threshold, hedgehogs retreat to the towns and villages, which act as refuges. And even in these ghettos, the abundance of hedgehogs depends on the density of the badger population nearby: the more badgers in the surrounding woods and fields, the fewer hedgehogs are squeezed into the suburban tapestry. The reason for this is thought to be the inability of young hedgehogs to disperse. Badgers catch and eat the youngsters, preventing movement and thus genetic flow within the hedgehog population. Suburban hedgehogs often become trapped within a ring of danger.

Now all this, though fascinating, might seem somewhat academic were it not for one thing: badgers are becoming more and more common. In Britain they increased by 10% from the 1980s to the 1990s, and the trend looks set to continue. With badgers on the up, the inevitable result will be a decrease in hedgehogs.

There will doubtless always be hedgehogs about. For whatever reason, there will remain some places where badgers occur at low density, not only in suburbia but also in other habitats where the spiny characters can thrive in their absence. Even so, researchers have been shocked in recent years to discover the impact of the one iconic species on the other. Certainly, the reality is a far cry from peace on the lawn.

Gardens are becoming ever more important sanctuaries for hedgehogs. Bread and milk is fine, but dog food makes a much better meal.

These Legs Were Made for Talking

IT'S HARD TO escape the reality of the dying summer in September, but there are a few garden creatures that help: the butterflies that flit about on the still-warm days, for instance, and the dragonflies that patrol the pond on their turbo-charged wings. Yet nothing, perhaps, is quite as consummately summery as the soporific chorus of grasshoppers and crickets. These sounds are the whispers that we hear as we settle in the long grass on a hot day, and they are the only songs that never quite stop on the warmest and muggiest nights.

Summer creatures they may be, but grasshoppers and crickets are tougher than they look and will serenade us right through the autumn to November, when the drone of flies has long died down and the whirr of wings has stilled. They are highly productive, these long-legged singers, and will spawn several generations over

this time. Any garden with a bit of long grass will do, and they need little invitation to stay. One species, the field grasshopper, has made a habit of colonising the central reservations of motorways. It is a flightless species, too, and one can only imagine the amount of hard hopping that must have taken place before the first pioneers made it, somehow, across the tarmac.

The legs of grasshoppers are indeed a marvel. These exceptional limbs, flexed like coiled springs, dominate their profile. Your average grasshopper can jump twenty times its own length in a single leap, and ten times as high as it is long – which is the rough equivalent of a human being clearing a five-storey building. The leg muscles develop a power that is equivalent to 20,000g per gram of its own weight, making it one of the strongest legs in the entire animal kingdom. And yet it is also a refined mechanism:

When you're a grasshopper, looking for a mate can be difficult in all that long grass.

the insect can crawl if required, it can make a modest leap and, when threatened, it can make a huge leap – way beyond the average predator's horizon.

Grasshoppers, not entirely surprisingly, live among grass. This is convenient enough for a creature that eats the stuff, as the grasshopper does, but it has its disadvantages when it comes to meeting a member of the opposite sex. Imagine trying to locate a partner among this towering forest of greenery: no wonder that, in our favourite fairytales, the princes have so much trouble when their princesses wander off into the forest. A few species of grasshopper do manfully keep on hopping and hopping until they find a female, but the majority resort to a quite different strategy: they sing.

Actually, 'song' is not quite the word for the sounds made by grasshoppers – although their relatives, the crickets, can be more melodic. In truth, most grasshoppers make rather dry noises: that of the common green grasshopper is described as 'a continuous chirp for 20 seconds or more', that of the field grasshopper 'a series of half-second chirps spread evenly over 12 seconds' and that of the meadow grasshopper (whoever named these creatures was not over-endowed with literary imagination) 'a burst of 10–15 pulses of ragged sounds, like a short, dry chuckle'. Nothing here to serenade yourself with over and over again, although it might be better than endless loops of Whitney Houston.

Nevertheless, the sounds do work, and they can carry a long way. They also have the advantage of being species-specific, thus avoiding accidental couplings between incompatible partners and red faces all round. Once a receptive female has heard the male's courtship song, she responds using a call of her own. The male enthusiastically replies and, little by little, the pair approaches one another. Once visual contact is made, they enter into an elaborate courtship routine that can involve many parts of the body and up to 20 different manoeuvres – the legs featuring prominently, of course.

But how do the male grasshoppers generate their songs in the first place? It turns out that each one is fitted with a number of small pegs or knobs on the inside of its hind femur, and generates the sound by rubbing the veins of its wings (even flightless species have the remains of wings) against these. This rubbing can be

The oak bush cricket signals for a mate by stamping its back legs.

exceedingly rapid: the common green grasshopper may strum its set of pegs 20 times a second. There may also be a considerable number of pegs. The field grasshopper has a mere 60–80, making it percussively somewhat limited, but several other species have at least twice this many and accordingly produce more complex and sometimes louder sounds.

Most grasshoppers actually have two kinds of songs, or 'stridulations' as they are more properly known. The male's summoning song, uttered to lure females, is the one we usually hear. Sometimes this is modified in rhythm a little, for example when males are intending to make insulting stridulations to one another. The other song, however, is the courtship song. This is done in the company of a receptive female, and can be highly elaborate. Quiet in nature, it is seldom audible to us.

The variety of sounds made by crickets is just as impressive as those made by grasshoppers, but these are produced by rubbing the wings together very fast, rather than by wings against legs. Cricket stridulations are more continuous and less staccato than those of grasshoppers, and, by contrast with the diurnal hoppers, they are usually heard at night. One species even eschews body-generated percussion entirely: the oak bush cricket, which is common in gardens, sits on the leaf-litter and stamps with its back legs, making a loud rustle that can be heard on the other side of the garden.

But whatever the preferred technique, one thing is undeniably true: among grasshoppers and crickets, it is very much the legs that do the talking.

119

SEPTEMBER, WITH ITS final flush of flowers and still warm days, could be seen as a dress rehearsal for autumn. But there's no mistaking the real thing now, as the temperature drops, the nights draw in and the trees drain the chlorophyll from the leaves. Yet this time of year has its own considerable bonuses. The huge crop of fruits and seeds is a chance to fatten up and plan ahead; it is like an offering to the garden's wildlife, wishing it well for the hard times ahead.

OCTOBER

Stocking Up and Caching in

AS A GARDENER it is hard not to lament the end of summer, with its days of fighting the growing lawn and admiring the blooms that have rewarded one's handiwork earlier in the year. And much of the garden wildlife, were it given to contemplation, would doubtless also wish the return of warm-season comforts, such as long days and buzzing insects. But these feelings are not universal. There are some animals for whom the summer is a drag and the autumn air is crisply satisfying and energising. Squirrels, especially, cheer at the return of the cold.

Squirrels may be opportunistic feeders, given to pilfering scraps from picnickers in city parks and bread from bird tables, but at heart they are lovers of tree seeds. For them, therefore, autumn is the season of plenty, with so much food around that they can satisfy themselves daily with the minimum of effort and strife. Indeed, in a normal year, within any relatively wooded suburb, the squirrels could not possibly hope to eat all the available food. It would be like a person discovering that all the food in the supermarket was free for a limited period: there would simply be far too much to take it all. This makes a big contrast with mid-summer, when seed production is just beginning and squirrels struggle to find anything much on the garden's 'shelves'.

In gardens with their favourite seed-rich trees, squirrels thrive. They simply wrap their paws around their food, and sink those powerful incisors into the target for which they have evolved. Few nuts escape their attention. Acorns, with their soft shells, are peeled by using the incisors like a tin-opener. Harder shells are held upright and split using the four incisors, two on the upper jaw and two on the lower, which bite into the top and then brings pressure to bear on the narrow edges until the two halves come apart. Conifer cones, with their built-in packaging that rivals the very worst in the supermarket toy section, are held much as we would hold a corn-on-the-cob, and munched until only the central core remains.

The seasonal nature of autumn's bounty does pose a problem, however. It may reach glut

It's a special garden that hosts red squirrels. But autumn sees these shy, uncommon creatures just as busy as their larger grey cousins.

proportions for a few months, but is then not replenished until the following year. In practice this may not be a problem until about February or March, because the trees distribute their crops so lavishly that secret corners of the garden usually still harbour stores of untouched nuts or seeds even after months of foraging by a variety of animals. Furthermore, some autumn fruits are long-lasting enough to provide useful nutrition at least six months later. So many vegetarian garden creatures can find food long after the autumn is forgotten – enough to get by from one day to the next.

However, there is a great deal more that a diligent squirrel can do to make its life easier in the early spring or during rough weather. When the food glut is still at its peak, it harvests and stores excess supplies away in a larder, to retrieve when times get harder. Anybody who has squirrels in their garden must have seen them engaged in this activity, which is known as caching. The squirrels take a few nuts or seeds in their teeth and then find a suitable patch of lawn or leaf-litter, whereupon they dig a shallow (2–3cm deep) pit with their front paws, drop the fruits inside and cover them up again, sealing the secret with a rub of the nose. It is all done with a minimum of fuss. Other seeds may be stored up in the trees, usually in small holes or fissures in the bark.

Importantly, no squirrel ever tries to store too many seeds away in a single cache. This would be foolhardy. The mantra of every independent financial advisor is to spread your investments wide, so that you are not vulnerable to single catastrophes; and the squirrels, even in the absence of IFAs, follow this wise practice. Therefore, even though an individual squirrel may store more than a thousand items away during the autumn, no single cache is likely to contain more than ten, and most contain just two or three. This spreading of assets is known technically as 'scatter-hoarding', and it serves the squirrels well.

Scatter-hoarding, however, has its snags. Apart from being hard work, and requiring both the space and the imagination to find hundreds of hiding-places, it also requires that the squirrels remember, when the need arises, exactly where all their valuable caches are located. In other words, they need a sort of mental filing system.

Although squirrels undoubtedly do uncover some caches by chance in the normal course of foraging – often picking up the precise location by scent – the experimental evidence strongly suggests that they generally remember the location of each cache, recalling the experience of burying it several months earlier. Scientific studies have shown that, even in areas where several squirrels have been hoarding in the same place, each individual shows a higher probability of finding its own than someone else's stores. Squirrels also tend, having homed in on an area, to move unhesitatingly from one cache to another one nearby. So it seems that their spatial memory is remarkably good. Thus, all their hard toil during autumn is not wasted.

Squirrels are not the only garden creatures that hide away their supplies. With the survival stakes so high, it is not surprising that other animals with the ability to do so have also taken to scatter-hoarding, including several of the garden's birds. Perhaps the best known of these is the jay, that colourful member of the crow family with its dazzling combination of black, white, pink and electric blue. Its autumnal collection tends to be dominated by acorns, and one individual may gather as many as 5,000 of these fruits in a single season. In contrast to squirrels, jays are territorial, and spend much of their time commuting between oak stands and their own territories. October is thus the best month to see these birds, as small groups travel with flopping flight just above the treetops, acorns held in bill and gullet. The nuthatch – a much smaller, short-tailed bird that creeps around tree trunks and branches – is also a great collector, although it tends to store its seeds in bark cracks up in the tree canopy. Nuthatches often raid supplies from bird feeders to build up their stores.

Down in the soil and leaf litter, rodents such as wood and yellow-necked mice are also collectors, albeit on a much smaller scale. You could call them scatter-hoarders, since they tend to use a number of sites, including under logs or in the crevices of walls or fences. By contrast with squirrels, however, these rodents routinely store large numbers of nuts in the safety of their nests, where the temptation to nibble them usually means that the stores don't last for long. Incidentally, recent studies on wood mice have revealed that, alone among all other known mammals except people, these rodents 'way-mark' their comparatively large territories by leaving strategic signs such as small twigs or leaves lying around. It is thus possible that they

A jay flies off to hide an acorn in its territory – just one of several thousand it will collect during the autumn.

'signpost' caches in the same way. Since wood mice are also known to find their way about by sensing the earth's magnetic field, it is hard not to conclude that these tiny rodents are rather brighter than they appear.

Ants and bees, of course, are also confirmed collectors of food. The colonies of some species are maintained throughout the winter without a universal die-off of workers and, not surprisingly, these animals also use the last bounty of autumn to build up reserves for the months ahead. The advantage for them is that colony activity is very low during cold weather, so quite limited reserves can be enough to ensure survival.

The great autumn swelling of the garden's supermarket shelves extends to everyone, of course, not just to those who would be prudent. Many gardens contain a variety of wild seeds, and one of the pleasures of the season is to watch the birds tucking in like Romans at a banquet, giving not a thought to the future. If your garden has thistles, lavender or teasels, for instance, you might well be visited by a flock of goldfinches. These fabulous birds, with their three-coloured heads and brilliant yellow wing markings, are highly adapted to extracting seeds from tight

seed-heads, such as those on thistles. They have thinner bills than most other seed-eaters and, interestingly, the stronger muscles in the jaw are those designed for opening, not closing the bill. This means that when a goldfinch inserts its bill between the bracts it can then open it *in situ* and squeeze out the seeds. Male goldfinches have fractionally longer bills than females (by a mere 1mm), which enables them to work teasel heads, while thistles are left to females.

The greenfinch, by contrast, has a bill that is robust enough to tackle sunflower seeds, and, indeed, it is the only finch that habitually does so. Yet this species is a versatile feeder and at other times – for instance, when working dandelion heads or chickweed – it can be the very essence of delicacy. Along with the blue tit, the greenfinch is also one of the few garden birds that will eat the seeds from rose hips.

The autumn is, of course, also the peak time of year for berry production. Although the best-known customers for these rich, nutritious seed-and-pulp sweeties are birds, a wide range of other garden animals, including mice, voles, squirrels and badgers, will also take them. Berries are wildly overproduced, in common with tree seeds, but differ from nuts and seeds in that they cannot be stored for long without spoiling. Thus, most berry eaters simply take as much as they can, when they can. The most obvious berry eaters in the garden are members of the thrush family, such as blackbirds and song thrushes, but plenty of others compete for them too, including starlings, woodpigeons and blackcaps.

As far as birds are concerned, berry abundance might be temporary, but it can still have lasting benefits. A few weeks of good eating can propel a bird into peak condition, which is especially important after it has just competed its annual moult and is in need of energy replenishment. By contrast with people, to whom binge eating can be extremely unhealthy, birds can only benefit when they are freed from the usual rigours and uncertainties of foraging. The berry crop may be temporary, but the birds' future survival chances will be enhanced by a good season.

For some garden creatures, the bounty of autumn produces important weight gain. Badgers, for example, eat more vegetable matter in the autumn than at any other time of year, and this helps them build up fat reserves for the leaner times ahead. If food becomes scarce later, these reserves are crucial – especially for the sows, which will become pregnant in the late winter. Thus from as early as July, badgers feed on grain from fields, and on nuts and berries. They will eat plenty of acorns, fallen clumps of elder- berries, yews, haws and, a par- ticular favourite, blackberries. So if you find any bushes that seem to have been emptied from the bottom up, this may be the work of badgers, which eat these succulent treats one by one, biting them off

individually. There is even a record of a badger that, frustrated in The *Fox and the Grapes* style, simply jumped off a bank and into the midst of a blackberry bush, its tough hide protecting it from the thorns as it contentedly plucked all the fruits that were now within reach.

Many other garden animals, from hedgehogs to queen bumblebees, put on weight to get through the winter. And, in a way, their strategy for survival is the same as that of the squirrels and jays. The latter store food in caches, the former store food as fat within their bodies. And while caches can be robbed, the same cannot be said of a plump badger, asleep on a cold night, its body replenished by the fruits of autumn.

This goldfinch is probably a male, since these are more able to extract seeds from teasel than females.

Silky Skills

A HEAVY AUTUMN dew reveals one of the garden's great secrets – albeit one that, although mostly unseen, has been there all along. The droplets of water vapour condense on the silk of spiders' webs, and suddenly the bushes, the grass and the garden's neglected corners are all draped with what looks washing hung out to dry by thousands of miniature householders. Only on these dewy mornings is it possible to appreciate just how many spiders there are in the world. They are everywhere: spinning, sitting, snaring, removing countless tiny invertebrates and putting credit into their account with gardeners.

So familiar are spiders' webs that we can easily forget how astonishing they are. For starters, we should not overlook the fact that, along with people and a few highly specialised insects, spiders are the only creatures that manufacture trapping devices at all. Their raw material, silk, is a complex protein with some remarkable properties. It happens to be the strongest natural fibre on earth and, while the 'average' strand is a mere 0.003mm in diameter, it can still trap and hold the body of a large struggling insect and withstand the full force of the buffeting wind. This is partly because, quite apart from being strong, it is also elastic. There must be plenty of possible uses for spider silk in human industrial systems, but the spiders just don't make enough of the stuff. Bully for them.

Although just about every species of web-making spider has its own specific web design (and many species, incidentally, make no webs at all), a close look around the garden will reveal three main types. The best known are those webs that you see suspended vertically between branches, or strung in front of gates and fences: these are known as orb webs. Peer into the corner of your shed and you will probably spot the second type, the sheet web. The builders of these horizontal webs hide themselves away in a dark passageway and run out when something blunders into their trap; they are often quite large, fast-moving and somewhat intimidating spiders. The last group includes those many webs that you can best see on the dewy ground on autumn days: these are known as space-and-scaffold webs, and tend to be a three-dimensional network of fibres attached either side of a more closely woven platform. They can also be found in bushes and shrubs, and can be very large. Interestingly, neither of these last two webs uses any sticky silk at all. The mesh of the platforms is enough to trip up any unintentional visitor, giving the fast-moving spiders time to close in on their prey.

However, perhaps the most pleasing constructions made by spiders are the orb webs. These represent the work of many different species, including the highly conspicuous, plump and intricately patterned garden spider. Since every garden has its population of garden spiders, it is this fine arachnid that can best teach us about the intricate task of web building and the rigours of web management.

If you wish to see a garden spider at work you could, I suppose, just mash up an existing web and watch the reconstruction, somewhat guiltily, at your leisure – though you should appreciate that building a web does take quite a lot out of its owner. Alternatively, you could try going into the garden in the morning when most webs are made, and sooner or later you will find one under construction. Either way, to observe the making of a web from its first stages to its last is one of the great privileges of being a garden wildlife enthusiast.

Spiders manufacture the silk in their bodies and then use their legs to pull it out, ready made, from several different ducts on their abdomen. (They are perfectly capable of pulling it from more than one duct at a time; they do have eight legs, after all). The trickiest part of web building is the beginning. The spider must try to fix two ends of a line of silk across a suitable space, like hanging a washing line. Starting at what will become a top corner, it will do one of two things: either it will attach some silk to the first point and crawl along to another at the same height, dragging the line behind it; alternatively, it will pull out a strand and leave it dangling for the wind to catch and whisk across the gap – a sort of passive version of throwing a grappling hook. Either way is fine, so long as the finished attached line is relatively level.

The next step is to repeat the first, but using a much slacker line, so that there are now two

Branch lines: the dew exposes the spider's trap

'washing lines' running next to each other across the gap, one taut and one slack. Once this is achieved, the spider ventures out to the centre of the slack thread and fixes a vertical line to it. It then lets itself down on this line, pulling the slack line taut into a 'V' and eventually making landfall on a point directly below, thereby completing a 'Y' of three radii. The middle of this 'Y', where the three lines meet, is now the centre of the web. The spider next adds more radii to the

'Y', until it starts to look like the spokes of a miniature bicycle wheel.

Next, the spider strengthens the web by laying strands of silk at right angles to the radii. It does this by fixing a line to the hub of the web and circling out in ever increasing spirals.

Now this is all very pretty, but the web is not quite ready to catch anything just yet: it is dry and trampoline-like, with no adhesive properties. For it to become an effective trap, the spider must now apply the sticky threads. In fact, it replaces the spiral strengthening thread with an adhesive thread, working from outside to in and actually consuming the strengthening thread as it goes. Its journey, and its labours, finish when it arrives back at the non-stick hub of the web. Here it takes a breather and waits for results.

This process might seem totally exhausting and time-consuming, and in many ways it is. The whole construction, from start to finish, occupies about an hour of the spider's time, which constitutes a larger proportion of its life than for those of us who are watching. But it is certainly time well spent: the builder is utterly dependent on its handiwork to supply its food.

Every construction requires maintenance, and spiders' webs themselves have a very short shelf-life, usually not much more than a couple of days. Bad weather may take its toll, but in fact it is dust and other debris collecting in the glue that is the real problem. Thus the spider routinely eats its own web and replaces it with another. It is a true craftsperson, working hard and true – and with no little panache.

All that hard work pays off.

The Visitors

HOW WELL DO you know the birds in your garden – not so much the different species, but the individuals? For most householders, especially if they put food out regularly, the answer is probably 'quite well'. Thus, once you've sprinkled some crumbs and nuts on the bird feeders, you can expect a visit from the garden robin, the garden's two blackbirds and perhaps a few blue and great tits. Who knows, perhaps the coal tit might pop in for a while, too? Every garden would seem to have its characters, part of the stable fabric of the garden scene.

In some instances, you could quite legitimately claim certain individual birds as 'your own'. Take the garden robin, for example. The bird that you see singing from the low shrub or sitting approvingly upon your idle spade, will very much be a resident and a familiar face. Robins are highly territorial in autumn, reserving spaces for their own ends and keeping private feeding spots. They react with great hostility to any intruders, chasing them away immediately – and these intruders, in turn, generally accept the birds' code of conduct by dashing from the scene of their trespass. Thus the garden robin you see in October will be the same robin that is still present in March, providing that it survives the winter. The same, incidentally, applies to another incendiary character, the wren.

Other garden birds, perhaps less welcome than robins or wrens, will also be long-term residents. For example, the house sparrow street gangs that invade your feeders are also very much local ruffians: sparrows live in small, stable colonies, with new recruits only being added in the early autumn, so the faces you see are familiar ones. The street pigeons – the ones with the varied plumage – are equally settled: the characters you see loafing on the roof will be

the very same from month to month and from year to year. And some other unpopular characters, including magpies and crows, live in stable pairs that occupy the same patch of ground all year round.

However, other faces may be less familiar than you might like to believe. Take the tits, for example. How many individual blue or great tits do you think visit your garden in a day or in a week? You might expect the answer to be ten or twenty, but it is probably many more than that. A study of one suburban garden where birds were being captured and colour-ringed concluded that about 70 individuals passed through in the course of a day, and more than 100 in a week.

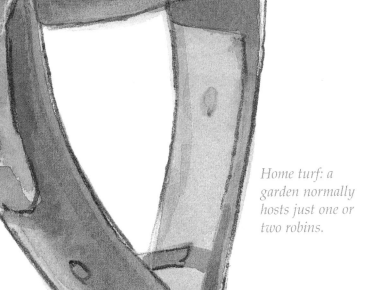

Home turf: a garden normally hosts just one or two robins.

These tits are interesting because they commonly make 'rounds' of a neighbourhood. By the middle of winter, birds have often settled into a daily routine, in which they might visit your garden for a few minutes at the same time each morning and then drop in on your neighbours' a little later – and perhaps your friends a few streets away towards evening. Since each bird will have its own routine, there will be a constant stream of individuals passing through during the day.

The situation is further complicated in tits because, during the course of a winter, the mix of individuals changes. Thus, while some birds remain in your neighbourhood, others live a virtually nomadic existence, seldom staying more than a few days at a given spot. Others are less mobile, but nonetheless begin to turn up in gardens as the winter progresses and the wild supplies of food elsewhere begin to dwindle. All in all, therefore, blue, great and coal tits all demonstrate a surprisingly fluidity in their populations.

At least most of the tits you see will have been hatched locally. But the population pattern in other birds can be very different. For example, where do you think that your blackbirds come from? The answer, in many cases, especially if just one or two come to the lawn, is that they will be locally born and bred. However, if you have several in your garden, say more than half a dozen, it is perfectly possible that some will be visitors from much further afield. We are not just talking about casual wayfarers here, but about complete foreigners. In the average autumn, a British garden will host at least some blackbirds from the Continent, originating from places such as Germany or Scandinavia. It is difficult to tell them from their local cousins, and thus they tend to melt, *incognito*, into the wintering population.

Blackbirds are not the only birds that exhibit this pattern. The same may also apply to song thrushes and chaffinches. Go down to your local park and feed the ducks: a good many will be foreign migrants, some from as far as Iceland. Watch the gulls flying over towards the local lake or reservoir in the evening: the majority will be not be British breeding birds.

The full extent of this foreign invasion is not widely recognised. But in the case of certain

Dozens of individual blue tits and greenfinches visit the garden daily.

Gulls flying to their evening roost: most will be foreign visitors.

Every garden birdwatcher's dream: the stunning waxwing.

birds, it is obvious they hail from elsewhere. Several superb, crisply plumaged species adorn our gardens in winter that we most certainly don't see in the summer. These include two smart species of thrush, the streaky-plumaged redwing and the frosty-backed fieldfare, species that travel together in flocks and often make a sudden and wholesale windfall on our unsuspecting property. Another delightful visitor is the delicate siskin, a small finch that does breed in Britain but occurs in much greater numbers in Scandinavian spruce forests, which is where most of our winter population has come from. Yet another is the brambling, a chaffinch-like bird whose plumage is washed through with that vivid orange so characteristic of autumn beech leaves. And – who knows? – you might even receive a state visit from the crown prince of unusual and exotic birds, the silky plumaged waxwing. There can be no doubt that this bird looks out of place in a humble garden. And it doesn't stay long: after guzzling its fill of berries – up to 600 a day – it will disappear into the endless winter landscape as suddenly and mysteriously as it arrived.

So, let's face it, with superstars like these liable to drop in at any moment, who cares whether the birds in the garden are 'ours' at all?

The Flip Side of the Menu

WHEN YOU LOOK over the autumn garden and muse on what its wildlife might be eating, most of the possibilities are obvious. Those bees and wasps that remain are feeding on nectar and pollen, while most of the birds and mammals are feasting on nuts, fruit and berries. One look at the garden spider's webs reminds us that a frightening percentage of our creatures actually eat one another.

But what other more unusual items might serve as food for our wildlife? When we have gone through the obvious favourites on the front of the menu, what remains on the back?

One particular product that is just coming into abundance at this time of the year, and which flourishes most sumptuously in the damp months of November and December, is fungi. But this food remains of relatively limited appeal, with rather few creatures feeding on it as a first choice. Virtually no birds eat the fruiting bodies, for instance, which seems odd, given how delicious we find them. One outstanding exception, however, is the red squirrel – if you are fortunate enough to have these glorious animals in your garden. Admittedly, most squirrels have eyes only for nuts at this particular time, but if the autumn has yielded a poor crop, red squirrels make for the treetops and harvest arboreal fungi, even storing some away for retrieval later in the winter. They form a nutritious second best to nuts and seeds. Other mammals, including bank voles, wood and yellow-necked mice, and occasionally even roe deer, will take fungi as part of their general diet, but seldom in prodigious quantities.

It is only invertebrates that really throw themselves at the fruiting bodies of fungi (unless you count fairies, which dance around them). Among the true enthusiasts are slugs and snails: a single large slug can consume a fruiting body on its own in an orgy of munching. The other major fungus-eaters are beetles, many of which are highly choosy about the type they eat – some being confined to a single species. Larger beetles can rival slugs in the amount they consume at a time. Both adults and larvae eat the flesh, and some of the longer-lasting fungi, such as the bracket-fungi found in trees, can give larval beetles the perfect well-fed start in life.

If the garden were a specialist restaurant, one

Slug palate: these molluscs like nothing better than the fruiting bodies of fungi.

An ant shepherd tends its flock.

of its signature dishes would be a product that a good many gardeners have never even heard of: honeydew. This sweet concoction is essentially the waste product of aphids and certain other juice-sucking insects, ejected as these tiny insects feed on the sap-transporting vessels of plants (the phloem). It is an abundant and evidently quite delicious product, which often crystallizes on the surface of stems and is evidently as sugary and light as candyfloss.

What makes honeydew so terrific is that it is not just sap, but refined sap. The drinking aphid requires many nutrients from its meal, and in order to balance its diet it must get rid of excess sugar, together with its other waste products. In fact 90% of the sugars go straight through an aphid's system, which means that honeydew is extremely energy-rich. It is also easy to find, and an impressive array of flies, wasps, bees, beetles and even some vertebrates willingly tuck in to supplement their diet.

Some ants, however, don't wait to find honeydew; they appropriate it straight from the aphids themselves, treating the sap-suckers like domestic animals. This association, known as ant-attendance, is of mutual benefit – although only just. The ants most certainly protect their domestic aphids from voracious predators such as lacewings and ladybirds, but they are overbearing and untrustworthy minders. They are also frequently predators of aphids, and their husbandry will often turn into exploitation: if the aphids are producing poor-quality honeydew, for example, the ants will sometimes just turn and eat the bugs instead. Fascinatingly, ants sometimes give the aphids another chance to get it right by transporting them, bodily, to another, more succulent part of the plant. Incidentally, the ant does not wait for the honeydew to be deposited on the plant stem, but actually drinks it straight from the aphid's anus.

The idea of eating another animal's waste products, or indeed your own, may not sound very pleasant, but this food source offers wholesome sustenance to many garden residents. Coprophagy – the consuming of faeces – is quite widespread and perfectly respectable among many animals, including rabbits. Being herbivores, rabbits eat plenty of material that is difficult to digest and, in order to extract all the possible nutriment, they make sure some of it passes through their digestive system twice. Last night's faeces are often eaten in the morning, when you and I are tucking into our porridge or cereal. Shrews, rather revoltingly, often lick theirs straight from the anus.

Of course, some invertebrates make a career out of eating what others have discarded, and although we may view these creatures with a degree of revulsion, we actually owe them our thanks. Nobody would like to live knee-deep in dung, so the army of flies, maggots, worms and dung beetles that perform this dirtiest of work with selfless relish actually help to keep our gardens clean and fresh. We don't have to make friends with them, just appreciate what they do.

THERE'S NO MISTAKING the winding-down atmosphere in the garden: the vegetation is tired, and the last leaves lollop exhaustedly to the ground. But the garden creatures have no time to follow suit. The winter is approaching, and most of them still have much preparation to complete before they can face the teeth of the cold.

NOVEMBER

Late autumn nightcap: a queen wasp, a red admiral and a comma have a last drink before hibernating, while a blackcap tucks into the last of the small insects.

Makeovers

IN NOVEMBER THE garden can look tired and messy, despite the best efforts of the keenest of gardeners. The ground is often sodden, and the constant battle against fallen leaves usually ends in defeat (which is just as well, because the leaves are good food for grateful earthworms). The last remaining flowers share their stems with shabby neighbours, and the trees have not yet shed enough leaves to expose completely their neat, stark winter skeletons. For the gardener, it is time to take a breather, and to contemplate tasks for the future.

The contrast between the garden itself and its residents, however, could hardly be starker. Most of our wildlife, individually speaking, looks simply magnificent. The coats of foxes, badgers and squirrels are luxuriant and smart, while the birds have barely a feather out of place. Even the few remaining invertebrates, such as red admirals and queen wasps, look brilliant against the backdrop of dark green ivy and soft autumn colours. Everything seems to look at its best.

This impression, in some ways, conveys a fundamental truth. Autumn has been kind and productive for many species, allowing them to put on weight and get into condition for winter. The fox's coat, for example, is every bit as thick and snug as it looks. These animals have spent much of the summer looking painfully scruffy, with bits of fur missing and their tails resembling worn-out brushes. Now, with their moult just completed – it lasts several months – the coat is ready for the cold season, and the fox's tail is the burning, red-brown poker that it ought to be. The hairs on the pelage (the technical word for a coat of fur) are as much as 5cm long, and so thickly spaced that, whatever the rigours of winter, the fox is unlikely to feel much cold. These marvellous predators are among the most impervious of all garden animals to winter; thick hairs, a catholic diet and their famed adaptability and craftiness see to that.

Badgers follow the same moulting course as foxes, with a summer moult producing a sumptuous winter coat. In this case, however, the hairs

In winter, the pied wagtail replaces its smart black bib with a smudgy serviette.

are even longer than those of the fox: up to 10cm, which is a couple of centimetres longer than those it has just moulted. The long, outermost guard hairs, which give the badger its silvery-grey coat (the summer coat is darker), are the first to re-grow, followed by the thick under-fur. The moult begins at the back and works its way forward, being completed round about now, in mid-autumn.

Winter is a less active season for badgers than for foxes, with long periods of almost compete dormancy when worms are scarce, so badgers need extra protection in the form of fat. This ensures that in December, when activity almost grinds to a halt, they can live off their bodily reserves. Fat is perfect for winter fuel because it can be stored dry, it yields more energy per unit volume than carbohydrate, and it can be laid down in layers under the skin. A winter badger is a heavy badger: the average spring weight is about 9kg, but this shoots up to 12kg in the autumn and can exceed 13kg. Sows, which will become pregnant before the winter is over, need to lay down more fat reserves than boars.

Squirrels have also finished their moult now, and are sporting thick winter coats. One way in which they differ from the carnivores mentioned above, however, is that these rodents have two moults a year, one in the spring and one in the autumn. The autumn moult progresses from back to front, finishing on the head. As with the fox, the most obvious beneficiary of this makeover is the tail, which turns from a tatty apology of a limb to a thick, dense flag that the animal can flaunt proudly among the branches. In red squirrels, a summer moult also does wonders for their designer ear-tufts.

While foxes, squirrels and badgers at best differ subtly in appearance between spring and winter, some garden birds undergo a complete makeover in autumn and can look very different indeed. In common with squirrels, birds generally moult twice a year. As well as allowing them to grow a thicker insulating covering of feathers, this is also an opportunity to change their colours and patterns from one season to the next, according to requirements. Thus, for example, pied wagtails have bold black breasts and throats in spring and summer, which play a part in enhancing their courtship routine; in winter this is reduced to nothing more than a dark band, like a serviette.

Some birds achieve their new look by a brilliantly economical process. The male chaffinch, for instance, sports a bright blue-grey head and pink flushed breast in spring, to replace the dull grey and wan brown of autumn and winter. This change is not down to replaced plumage, but rather to wear and tear. You see, the new feathers produced in autumn have dull-coloured tips, with brighter colours lying just beneath. So as the winter drags on and the feathers are weathered, the tips erode, revealing the colourful section of each feather just in time for spring, when the sexes awake to the idea of breeding. Much the same happens with the starling. Autumn starlings sport dark plumage with white spots. These spots wear away as the season progresses, leaving the iridescent tips to shine brightly and beguile those that matter.

Of course, donning a new coat of fur and feathers is a superficial change that goes no further than skin-deep. But far more profound changes are taking place for many garden creatures. The ultimate makeover, as it were, must be metamorphosis. We cannot produce a TV show in which a member of the public is genuinely transformed from frog into prince, for instance, but for many invertebrates a

Seasonal turnaround: the grey squirrel's thin summer coat (right), with wispy tail, is replaced in the autumn (left) with a thick, bushy coat.

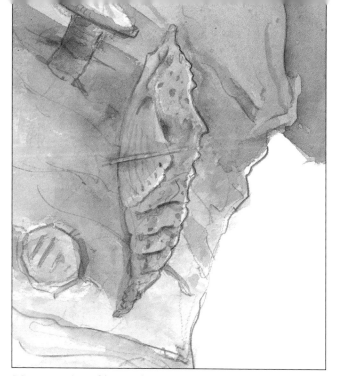

change of this magnitude is routine. For the average butterfly or moth, subsisting as it does on the nectar of flowers, survival during winter as a motile adult would usually be impossible. But as a dormant chrysalis, protected by a tough outer layer, and often buried in the earth or among the leaf litter away from the cutting teeth of frost, it has a chance. Similarly, many other invertebrates enter some kind of immature stage during the cold season. Various flies and beetles, along with butterflies and moths, will overwinter as either pupae, larvae or, in the ultimate state of shutting down, eggs. During this stage, whichever it may be, they enter a state of developmental arrest known as diapause, which is equivalent to hibernation in higher animals. This makes them remarkably tolerant of cold, and certain insects can even survive the freezing of some of their internal tissues. Many withstand temperatures well below freezing, since various body chemicals prevent their internal temperature from falling that far.

… while others, such as these small tortoiseshells, remain in the adult stage, finding a cosy spot in which to become dormant.

Not all invertebrates pass the winter in this clandestine way, however. Indeed, a few garden butterflies (peacock, red admiral, small tortoiseshell, comma and brimstone) will seek a hideaway in the adult form and remain dormant, awakening with fine weather in the spring. Furthermore, many invertebrates that live in the soil will be quite immune to the season, insulated from frost and carrying on life as normal. And then there are others, such as honeybees, that neither change their bodies nor dive into dormancy. These animals practise a different kind of makeover: they alter their environment.

Admittedly, the alteration is behavioural rather than structural. During winter, the bees gather together in a large, three-dimensional cluster inside their hives in order to keep themselves warm. Those on the inside eat honey and, suitably energised, they begin to beat their wings very fast without actually taking off. This manoeuvre, which is equivalent to shivering, generates considerable heat. The heat is maintained at the centre of the cluster by the insulating bodies of those on the outside. A continual rota system ensures that every bee takes its turn at both inside and outside duties (and those in between) and thus everybody benefits. Astonishingly, this regimented behaviour ensures that the temperature in the cluster centre is maintained at close to 30°C.

Warm winter hideaways

For other garden creatures, less spectacular but equally substantial changes to their living quarters help them combat winter cold. Once again, a good example of this is seen in squirrels. These animals make two types of 'home': dreys, which are the well known nests that you can see among the branches of trees; and dens, which are made in tree-hollows and many squirrel watchers have never actually seen. The structures differ from summer to winter, with the winter nests, unsurprisingly, being more robust and weatherproof.

Dreys look similar to the nests of birds – although they are a lot bigger than most; only the magpie's domed structure comes close, but is not as dense and contains fewer leaves. They are generally placed in sheltered treetop locations, often against a fork or in the crown of a conifer, and are rarely lower than 5m above ground. Winter dreys are made up from various twigs that the squirrels bite off, large at first when the initial

A squirrels' winter drey is a robust structure, and needs to be.

platform is being built, and then smaller and more refined as the builders start to add the finishing touches to make the nest weatherproof. They are lined with anything soft, including moss and feathers, to add a little extra comfort.

Hedgehogs also build nests, and theirs are even more vital for survival than those of squirrels, since for most of the winter the owner will be in the vulnerable state of hibernation. These prickly insectivores go to great lengths to pile up grass and leaves under some kind of shelter, and then bury themselves deep within the pile, thus becoming both sheltered and camouflaged. The covering of vegetation also enables them to keep the temperature above freezing.

Compared to a badger's sett, the nest of a squirrel is no more than a flimsy bivouac. The badger is one of the largest underground living animals in the world, and its complex, labyrinthine

Bedding down: badgers preparing for those chilly winter nights.

tunnel systems are like palaces. There are various records associated with badger setts: they can reach depths of up to 4m; they can be wide enough for a person to crawl in (usually about 25cm wide and 30cm high); a single system can incorporate 300m of tunnels, and so on. Larger setts, which can have many entrances, boast all sorts of mod cons, including annexes, side-burrows, breeding and resting chambers. Not every sett has been completely investigated, so perhaps one day someone will discover snooker tables and satellite TV down there. Whatever its particular refinements, a badger sett adds up to a stable environment and a thoroughly pleasant place to be on a cold day. Unsurprisingly, it usually attracts a wide range of other tenants.

However, a spacious sett alone is not enough for the fastidious badger. It also requires bedding – and lots of it. Thus, if you watch badgers at their sett entrances at this time of the year, you might well observe some bedding collection in progress. Dry grass and hay are always popular materials, and dead bracken is a seasonal must-have for the discerning carnivore. The bedding is collected from as far away as 80m, which shows just how important it is. The badger bundles up its load, stuffing it between forepaws and chin, then drags it backwards – often surprisingly quickly – toward the sett.

On a much smaller scale, mice also build nests and live in underground burrows, although a human would certainly have great trouble trying

to crawl into one of their chambers. By contrast with badgers, mice also use their residences as food stores, and thus may remain more or less active throughout the cold season. Mice being mice, they might still be breeding even at the start of winter.

Of all the creatures that you might expect to build winter nests, birds must come top of the list. Yet they rarely bother. They might sometimes use nests for roosting, but, these are usually ones that have been made by other species. Thus sparrows may roost in old house martin nests and other smaller birds in crow's nests, and all sorts of birds that don't normally nest in holes will use tree holes or nest-boxes. There are a few exceptions: owls sometimes roost throughout the year in a chamber that they might also use for breeding, and woodpeckers may make a winter hole that later becomes a nursery. But for most birds, no nest is needed in winter. Their original body makeover, a few layers of extra feathers, is preparation enough.

Tawny owls may live in the same hole all year round.

Ladybird, Ladybird, Fly Away Home

IT IS NOW late autumn, and indeed all the ladybirds should have flown home. This is no time to be an insect, with the cold and the damp prevailing, and the summer a distant memory. Any sensible insect should be a pupa, a larva or an egg by now.

But ladybirds are clearly not sensible. In fact, they are among just a handful of insects to spend the winter out of the soil and in the adult stage. By vernacular description, therefore, they are hibernators, although technically they only remain dormant, since true hibernators are animals that can regulate their own body temperature. Whatever the language, everyone agrees that ladybirds do their sleeping in style.

What is so striking about the ladybirds' long winter nap is the way in which they do it in clusters. The number of individuals concerned varies from species to species. Most gatherings contain just a handful, but several species routinely cluster in the tens, some in the hundreds and one species, the sixteen-spot ladybird, sometimes in thousands. Inevitably, in North America, where people always have to do things bigger, up to 100,000 have been found

together. But any gathering of these colourful insects can be a profoundly impressive sight, as their markings seem to multiply them. And as if to add a flourish of design, some of the larger assemblages contain several different species, as though these beetles were trying to play dominoes together.

The places where ladybirds cluster – their hibernacula – vary, as do the aggregate scores, although they always choose sheltered spots, out of the worst of the wind or rain. Several species, including the ten-spot ladybird and the fourteen-spot ladybird, hide away in the leaf litter on the ground, while others use stems or the dead foliage of plants such as thistles. However, the most interesting locations as far as gardeners are concerned are those chosen by two-spot lady-birds, because these insects often find the insides of houses or outbuildings (including greenhous-es) irresistible. And who can blame them? Their aggregations are sometimes surprisingly obvious – along a window-frame, perhaps – while they also creep into piles of papers, logs or old rags. In fact, finding several hundred unexpected ladybirds in such places can be quite a shock.

But why cluster, you might ask, when you can snuggle into a quiet crevice by yourself? The answer has proved surprisingly abstruse. The most persistent theory is that clustering offers a form of defence against predators. There is as yet no conclusive proof of this, but it does make sense. Ladybirds have what is known as aposematic coloration, meaning that their bright colours warn predators that they are unpalatable. The presence of so many together must serve to magnify this effect and thus help protect the insects from disturbance. There is one potentially serious disadvantage, though, since large gatherings of insects are uniquely vulnerable to the spread of disease.

Nonetheless, the ladybirds stick rigidly to their overwintering habit, and to their hibernacula. The same locations tend to be used year after year, being passed down the generations, since few ladybirds live long enough to overwinter more than once. It seems that they find their way to the correct sites using some kind of scent, although it is not known what chemical this is. Deepening the mystery is the fact that different hibernacula host somewhat different survival rates, which raises a question over why the individuals use the more dodgy ones in the first place. In general, though, the overwintering habit clearly works, because in a mild season up to 90 per cent of dormant ladybirds will survive. Once they awaken in the spring, some will have been dormant for more than eight months, which puts quite a strain on their body chemistry.

Not surprisingly, the newly awakened sleepers make up for lost time and are soon reproducing wildly. A single ladybird female can lay several hundred eggs, which, curiously, are almost always yellow. Apart from their fashion sense, there are several other aspects of the ladybirds' breeding cycle that are also distinctly quirky. First, the female ladybird will regularly copulate far more often than is necessary for fertilisation – in fact, up to ten times as often. It is thought that she does this to ensure that, with many different males contributing sperm, there is a wide genetic diversity within her clump of eggs. Thus, at least some of the hatchlings should be predisposed to whatever habitat they find themselves in.

Another possibility is related to sperm competition. Female ladybirds store all the sperm they receive from every male in a single organ known as a spermatheca. Once ready to fertilise the eggs, they open the spermatheca and the sperm are then locked in a hundred-metre dash to fertilise. Only the best win, with the result that the eggs will be fertilised by the best quality genetic material. It's an ingenious strategy, yet it seems that males have cottoned on to the potential disadvantages: their sperm-holding organs, the spermatophores, contain so much sperm that they almost fill the female's spermatheca and, during copulation, can thus flush out the sperm of those who have gone before. No doubt this is all part of the battle of the sexes. The only trouble with the ladybirds' promiscuity is that, believe it or not, they suffer from sexually transmitted diseases.

Yet another quirk of ladybird reproduction, and indeed ladybird life, is that adult and larval stages can be cannibalistic. This happens most often among the larvae, and, hardly surprisingly, tends to occur most frequently when there aren't enough aphids to keep the little monsters fed. But it is also known among adults, with adults of one species eating adults of another – or even of their own kind.

And that's a disturbing thought. What if something goes horribly wrong at the hibernaculum? Ladybird, ladybird, will you sleep easy tonight?

The Strange Case of the Fox and the Footwear

OF ALL THE relationships between animals and people in the garden, none is quite so fractious, or emotionally charged, as that between the town-dweller and the fox. And equally, no relationship has changed so much, from what was mainly outright hostility fifty years ago to the respect and sometimes affection we see today. If a single fox had lived for that span of fifty years, it would shake its greying head and marvel at it all.

A principal reason for this change has been the fox's successful colonisation of our own suburban habitat. Nowadays it is much easier to see an urban fox than a country fox. These canny predators are firmly established in the leafier suburbs of most British cities, and it should no longer be a surprise to find them lurking among us.

There is one sure sign that the relationship between foxes and people has reached a comfortable familiarity: we have come to learn some of the fox's odd habits, just as they have come to learn some of ours. That's one of the things about cohabiting: the veneer of respectability falls away and those personal quirks and traits are bound to show their face. Perhaps your flatmate wakes up in the middle of the night to eat jam and peanut-butter sandwiches, or perhaps your spouse never goes out before a round of watering all the house plants – that sort of thing. It's the kind of behaviour that can be an irritation at first, but which we gradually come to accept as a harmless eccentricity.

(Above, right and opposite above) A fox is sorely tempted by the sight and smell of shoes, especially leather ones. This violated footwear is unlikely to be worn again.

And foxes certainly do have several eccentricities, of which one of the oddest has to be their preoccupation with shoes. These are not foxy shoes, you understand, but human shoes. Our shoes. Given half a chance, the canny canines simply won't leave them alone. If you forget to take your footwear in from the garden at night, you have made a mistake: you are quite likely to find it strewn around in the morning, probably chewed beyond repair, perhaps adorned with faeces and undoubtedly covered with the pungent odour of the perpetrator. There is no doubt that your footwear has featured strongly in the fox's night-time entertainment.

But why should a fox be so interested in shoes? There are several obvious reasons. First, the shoes have their own inherent smell, especially if they are made from leather. Even we humans love the scent of new boots or brogues, so to a fox, for whom all smells are magnified, the scent is clearly even more irresistible. And then, of course, we put our feet in them as well, adding our own odour to the mix. Shoes are thus a pungent pot-pourri of marvellous smells, none of which is

familiar to a garden animal and must be thrillingly novel. Just as we, who are most stirred by visual cues, can admire a painting or a landscape, so a fox is equally excited by its olfactory environment.

Another attractive aspect of shoes is that they are just the right size and texture for foxes to chew on. With plenty of give around the ankles, contrasting with hard leather around the toes, they make the ideal work-out for the jaws. Most shoes are light enough to shake and carry about, too, so they can serve as toys in games. All in all, human footwear might almost have been designed with the delight of foxes in mind.

Not surprisingly, the habit has brought foxes into conflict with some people. One particular South London street recently suffered a spate of footwear thievery, many of the stolen goods being brand-new and treasured by their human owners. In Melbourne, Australia, which calls itself the fashion capital of the country, concern about shoe-loving foxes has reached the pages of the press, and the phenomenon has been coined 'Imelda Syndrome' after the notoriously shoe-obsessed wife of the late Philippines president Marcos.

In fact, footwear is not the only human product that fascinates foxes. They have also been seen playing with childrens' toys – especially soft toys (no one has yet seen a fox using a Playstation), while gardening gloves, handbags and balls are also frequently abused. The latter, it could be argued, may well attract attention by resembling birds' eggs, and this is particularly true of golf balls. Indeed, some tournament officials in Sweden faced an unusual problem recently when a fox took players' balls in the middle of play and they were unsure of how to keep the score. (I suppose it depends on whether foxes could be classed as spectators.) This should come as no surprise, since golf courses, with their rough corners and undisturbed habitat close to human settlement, make excellent hideaways for foxes.

A golfer on the round of his or her life might become very irritated by the thieving of a ball on a perfect lie, but for most people the idea of foxes interrupting golf is merely funny. However, a few foxes have developed a habit that just about any victim would find annoying: the miscreants take clothes from washing lines. In doing so they are, of course, quite unaware of the sensibilities of the owners, and will see to it that nearby gardens receive offerings of underwear and other garments that were best left inside the home. The attraction must, once again, be primarily one of smell. If we enjoy that just-washed scent, we can be sure that it is also a powerful stimulus for such an olfactory operator as a fox. Washing flapping in the wind, especially bright white clothing, is also visually appealing.

Thus the suburban landscape, although it provides many challenges for a fox, must also be a uniquely fascinating place to live for a relatively intelligent animal, offering a bombardment of novel stimuli. No wonder foxes do so well here. However, one thing must keep them wondering: with the strange smelly objects they collect, and their bizarre practice of covering up their bodies, hands and feet, those human beings really are an eccentric bunch of animals.

Foxes find human artefacts fascinating.

In the Golden Pond

IF YOU HAVE a pond in your garden, you will know that it is a community within a community. The rain falls on lawn and pond alike, as do the golden leaves of autumn. But that does not mean they are the same. Indeed, the pond reacts slightly more slowly to the cold season than the air above, which means that, in November, the pond can still be a hotbed of activity while the rest of the garden descends into torpor. The waters of the pond hold plenty of intrigue yet, and many of its creatures, even the insects, remain fully active all year.

Mind you, the overall rules of the pond are much the same as in the soil, the grass or the leaf litter. A male frog might slip slowly down into the mud at the bottom and spend its winter blissfully torpid, but for much of this watery world the same laws of 'eat or be eaten' apply at this time as much as any other. Danger is everywhere. The food chains are the same, although the characters are different.

One of the most intriguing aspects of pond life is that the predatory underworld, that guild of creatures that terrorise the rest by stalking them unto death, is dominated by, of all things, bugs. These are not 'bugs' in the very general sense of the word – the one that describes all creepy crawlies – but very specific bugs: the Hemiptera. They are a bit like beetles, and their best-known representatives are aphids. If it is difficult to imagine an aphid as frightening, then consider what aphids do: with their sharp mouthparts, these minute insects penetrate the tough stems of plants and suck out their fluids. From here it is not a big step to penetrating the hides of other creatures and systematically sucking them dry.

Thus, throughout the pond habitat, there are mouthparts ready to do just that, and the bugs that wield them live both below and above the water surface. Those above are particularly insidious, perhaps because they look somehow harmless. Take the pond-skater. This insect is as elegant as a ballet dancer, with its spindly, evenly splayed legs and its pencil-thin body, and it skips across the pond supported by just a narrow film of surface tension. The pond skater preys mainly upon insects that become waterlogged, cutting short their drowning with the lethal incision of its jaws. Thus this skater is more Tonya Harding (the American who had her rival beaten up by hired thugs) than Torvill and Dean.

Floating just below the surface, but with the same unsympathetic outlook towards struggling insects, is the water boatman. This insect is more quirky than elegant, having a keel-shaped dorsal surface and legs that stick out like oars. Holding an air-bubble on its front, it navigates the water surface by backstroke, which means that its fearsome mouthparts face upwards. This is another uncompromising predator, which makes a meal of everything from drowning insects to aquatic colleagues, including water fleas and sometimes small fish. It even attacks human fingers when they get too close, giving a powerful enough bite for us to recoil with the pain.

The bug mafia operates under the water, too. Here lurks the scariest of the trio of assassins, the water scorpion. It does indeed look a little like a

The water scorpion's 'tail' is actually a breathing tube.

Surface tension: a pond skater waits for small insects to fall into the water, before pouncing.

scorpion, with its long 'tail' (actually a breathing tube that remains open to the air even when the rest of the animal is submerged) and pincers. The latter have developed into what look like muscle-bound arms, and they hold any victim long enough for the mouthparts to finish it off. Water scorpions are slow-moving creatures that lie among the mud or weed all year long, ambushing whatever bumbles past.

But not all the pond's bugs are murderous. The lesser water boatman is an insect that more closely resembles conventional oarsman by rowing around the right way up. This blameless creature eats nothing much more than algae and other plant debris, which enables it to be active all year long. In contrast to the water boatman, it often dives below the surface, breathing from the bubble of air that it holds to its chest. In spring, a male serenades a female by rubbing its hairy front legs against a ridge on its face, stridulating like an underwater grasshopper.

Of course, there are plenty of other active animals in the pond besides bugs, and many dangers lie in wait for the small, aquatic and edible. Water beetles, whether larval or adult, have the habit of liquidating most of their aquatic colleagues in the confines of a small pond; they are like the perpetrators of the killing on a murder mystery weekend, when all the guests are confined to a house and begin to drop, one by one. Alongside these, the larvae of dragonflies are just as fearsome, and you do begin to wonder why anything dares to live underwater at all.

There are grazers here, too, including several species of snail, notably the great pond snail and the ramshorn snail. Both spend their time harmlessly munching algae and other plant debris. The latter has the distinction of haemoglobin in its blood, which might perhaps add a bit of colour to the general carnage.

But if you are really after action in your pond, then look no further than that strange assortment of creatures that go by the tag of bugs.

DECEMBER ALWAYS HAS
the scruffy feel that you might expect
from a year dragging towards its
end, and in the garden it can be a
quiet month. But it is also the month
when the gardener, by feeding and
leaving undisturbed corners, can
make a genuine contribution to
the survival of many visitors.

DECEMBER

Pride and Prejudice

THERE CAN BE few more obvious signs of a wildlife-friendly household than a bird feeder placed in the corner of a garden. Recent estimates suggest that there is one bird-table for every three homes in Britain, which suggests a total figure of about 15 million. That is enough to constitute a cultural phenomenon, part of the shifting sand of modern living. In fact, with the practice of eating on the sofa or at the desk becoming more and more common, and the model of the nuclear family under increasing challenge from alternative social structures, there could soon be more bird-tables in this country than dinner tables. It is a striking endorsement of our collective love of, and fascination with our garden wildlife.

Yet the bird feeder can also illustrate both our ambivalence towards wild creatures and their ambivalence towards us. For their part, birds have no feelings toward human beings, except fear and suspicion. They rarely enter our houses and most flee at the very sight of us, but they undoubtedly benefit from the provision of food, and some become entirely dependent on our handouts. And as for us, the bird-table can be a place where – alongside a heart beating for wildlife – our prejudices proliferate. The honest householder may take pride in looking after birds, showing them a devotion that outdoes some of their human relationships, yet may still harbour a grudge against certain characters.

Take pigeons. These are wild birds that, in common with some smaller species such as sparrows or tits, are regular visitors to bird tables, taking seeds and grain. Yet most householders don't like pigeons. They complain that these large birds take 'more than their fair share' and that they keep other smaller birds away from the feeding site. At the same time, these very same householders delight in the energetic antics of tits and their frenetic visits to the feeders.

Clearly this is an absurd position. As wild birds, both pigeons and tits should be equal before the householder, since both are taking advantage of the same food resource for the

same reason. There are no value judgments to be made between the two. People may complain that pigeons monopolise the resource to the exclusion of others, yet this is precisely what individual tits are doing. Within gatherings of tits there are hierarchies, and the dominant birds get more food than others. Indeed, one blue tit may well simply steal food from another of its kind or from a subordinate species such as a coal tit, yet we dismiss this bullying and theft as harmless jockeying at the feeders. Another much beloved species, the robin, is even worse, often violently expelling other individuals of its own kind, and even some other species, from its garden territory. Yet the pigeons, which do not

The ups and downs of life at the feeders make riveting drama. Here, a great tit looks for a way in among a gaggle of greenfinches.

Unwelcome visitors? Two woodpigeons tuck into some table food thoughtfully provided by the householder.

exclude any other species from their territory, suffer our prejudice, simply because they look more gormless than gorgeous.

This kind of prejudice isn't a crime, but sometimes it can have serious consequences, especially when it comes to the vexing matter of predation. Recent years have seen an outcry about magpies in gardens. These smart black-and-white crows are well known for raiding the nests of smaller and more 'lovable' species, such as blackbirds, and consuming the eggs and young – often right in front of horrified householders and the hysterical parent birds. It is a horrible sight, and one that nobody enjoys. Many, on observing this carnage, assume that the magpies must be harming the prospects of the wider bird community and stir themselves to sign petitions for the culling of the offender. And yet study after study has failed to link magpie predation to populations of any garden bird species. Magpies don't deter birds from entering the garden. Bird populations are fine and fickle things, and any number of factors can affect them. Yet many people choose to ignore this, and see red at the mere appearance of a magpie in the garden.

A similar case involves the sparrowhawk. People are often upset by the sight of this dashing predator snatching a small bird from their feeder, and some conclude that enough is enough

Sparrowhawks are unpopular for eating small garden birds. But, like prey, they need to eat.

and 'something must be done'. They fall for the persuasive folly of the 'cull it!' brigade, who never seem to realise that the very existence of a sparrowhawk is proof of a healthy small bird population, not an agent for its destruction. Sparrowhawks depend for their lives on small birds being abundant, and they feed on what scientists call the 'sustainable surplus' – i.e. that proportion of any population, often comprising the sick, weak or young, that will inevitably be lost to predation or other natural causes. It is ecological nonsense to suggest that their presence is a threat to garden bird populations.

Even more outrage is stirred over the subject of cats. It is in our gardens, away from the comfort of our houses, that the domestic cat reveals its true genetic inheritance. Put simply, it is a natural-born killer – and that, in a way, is part of its allure. Between them, cats are estimated to kill more than 20 million birds every year in Britain, which far exceeds any destruction wrought by magpies. And they kill mature breeding adults, too, which magpies almost never do. There is simply no question that our garden wildlife, which also includes mice, voles, shrews and frogs, would do better without cats – and, incidentally, without dogs, too.

But that isn't really the point. Nobody is ever seriously going to suggest that cats should be banned from our lives, nor dogs, nor rabbits, nor guinea pigs. What does matter, however, is the will of that cat-loving householder. Every garden belongs to somebody: it is a little fiefdom, where the decisions of the owner hold sway. In the end it matters less whether the owners have a love of cats than whether they have a heart for the general well-being of wildlife in the garden.

It is this that will determine the fortune of the creatures in a garden – and, ultimately, it can have a bearing on the national fortunes of some of our favourite species.

Gardening for conservation

It is easy to forget that, pooled together, gardens represent a major national habitat. In fact their overall area exceeds that of all Britain's national nature reserves put together. And one characteristic that nature reserves and gardens share is the need to be managed. Many people think that, if you are setting an area aside as a nature reserve, all you have to do is delineate it, keep the people out and let the wildlife get on with things. But our country hardly has a square inch of land that is perfectly natural – at least in the sense that it can be just left wild. The truth is that even the best, most wildlife-rich places are maintained and often even created by people. Take lowland heathland: this habitat – one of our most threatened, and home to many rare forms of wildlife found nowhere else – is fundamentally a human creation; without appropriate management it would cease to exist.

A few overgrown corners can transform a garden into a haven for wildlife.

The point is that, in a way, our gardens are little different from the larger protected areas out there, and can be quite reasonably maintained as small but authentic nature reserves. On our own patch, every aspect of our management – yes, our gardening – can be important in maintaining a place fit for wildlife.

One thing that used to distinguish the average garden from a nature reserve was that, on the whole, nature reserves harboured rare or special wildlife, while the garden merely housed the everyday and humdrum. This, though, is no longer the case. Sadly, the turnaround is not because strange and exotic animals are now being recorded in gardens (although this sometimes happens, especially among bats and moths), but more because formerly widespread animals are now declining in the countryside. These animals are fleeing the new environmental deserts of our rural landscape and taking refuge in gardens instead. Frogs, newts and toads, for example, used to abound in the little wet corners and ponds that dotted farmland but are now mostly gone; today these amphibians are easier to find in gardens than almost anywhere else. The same applies to slow-worms in garden rubbish heaps, and there is probably no easier place to see a grass snake than in a garden. Even some birds that are losing precious habitat elsewhere have started appearing more frequently in gardens, the bullfinch and reed bunting being good recent examples.

So gardeners are now responsible for some truly precious wildlife. Our efforts at maintaining a pleasant retreat at the back of our house have now become of great ecological importance, both individually and collectively. We are thus at the cutting edge of conservation. Read this book in the morning, and you can make a difference by the afternoon!

People are always asking how they can help garden wildlife, and there are already many excellent books devoted to the subject (see page 159), so I won't dwell on specifics here. However, a couple of points seem to be especially important and can be made with all wildlife in mind.

The first is that, as a general rule, chemicals are a bad idea. These include insecticides, herbicides and such things as slug pellets. Remember, your garden could offer a vital refuge for wildlife amidst the ecologic deserts of intensive farming, but it won't if you spray chemicals: that's just aping what they do on the farms. There are many reasons to desist. Take aphids. Yes, it is annoying that they cluster on your favourite blooms, and nobody is disputing the fact that they do cause

You might not like slugs, but hedgehogs most certainly do.

damage. But aphids are food for a wide variety of less destructive creatures, including ladybirds. If you can just hold back on the spraying and allow the aphid guzzlers to move in – or even bring in some ladybirds that you have found elsewhere in the garden or locally – then you might find that your worst fears are unfounded. The same applies to all kinds of chemicals: they are bound to be detrimental to your wildlife in the long term, perhaps in ways that you will never know. If you must use pest control, there are many techniques that do not cause harm, not least the fast developing range of organic products.

A second plea that I would make to all gardeners is to resist the siren call to tidiness and perfection. Yes, a tidy garden does look great, but isn't a garden full of wildlife even better? The fact is that, for wildlife generally, a little untidiness goes a long way. Undisturbed corners can be an excellent thing, offering homes to everything from woodlice to hedgehogs.

Of course, that does not mean that your garden should be scruffy, either, and it is not licence to quit the maintenance of your patch of ground altogether. Most gardens left entirely alone would simply become messy, unproductive habitats, growing too much grass and plenty of local resentment. What is required is a happy medium: not a wild garden, but a garden managed for wildlife.

Another issue that often arises is the matter of feeding your garden creatures. It has been suggested that the provision of food fosters unnecessary dependence of the wildlife upon you, the householder. Some go as far as to say that well fed animals in gardens are somehow second rate, having never learnt to fend for themselves properly, and constitute a sort of ecological underclass. On the whole, this seems to be largely untrue. You might think, for instance, that all your local hedgehogs make a bee-line every evening for gardens, but close study has shown

this not to be true. Hedgehogs are rather mature about the whole thing, treating gardeners' provision as a useful, though not essential, supplement to their normal diet. You might find foxes become a bit attached to you, but that is no crisis, either. They are just being opportunistic. Deprive them of their eatery for a few days, and they will soon move on to the rest of the neighbourhood.

If you are keen on feeding birds, there are some minor rules you should apply. Birds are creatures of habit, and often do become quite dependent on the food you leave out. So please do try to be reliable; don't put copious amounts out for a while, and then suddenly stop. Birds appreciate smaller, predictable helpings.

One of the many delights about a love for garden wildlife is that we really can help our wild neighbours, and how much we help depends on what we can afford and what our personal interests are. Catalogues these days are full of products that, only a few years ago, would never have been commercially viable. You can buy specialist bird foods or feeders for your favourites, and you can acquire everything from hedgehog boxes to breeding boxes for bumblebees. Many gardeners also plant especially for wildlife, introducing a berry-bearing shrub or a buddleia, guaranteeing further delights.

And delight is, in essence, the watchword for every keen wildlife gardener. To have a garden is a privilege. Properly managed, delight can be the happy by-product.

151

Remarkable Rodents

WHEN GARDEN WILDLIFE enthusiasts swap stories about their wild inhabitants, the conversation usually revolves around foxes, frogs or birds, with occasional helpings of butterflies or bumblebees. But what every gardener conspicuously avoids mentioning, as if it were too hot a topic or was somehow rather embarrassing, is rodents. Most of us just cannot seem to admit that we host mice or rats, even if the former are merely mild-mannered wood mice, found in every rural garden. And no wonder: one mention of these creatures is enough to set our neighbours' alarm bells ringing. Rodents ruin relationships.

It is said, though, that nobody in the world lives any more that a few metres from the nearest rat. This might be an exaggeration, but a genuine truth lies behind it: namely, that these rodents – both house mice and brown rats, to use their official species names – are everywhere. Yet it wasn't always the case. Both originate from Asia and, having arrived here on the coat-tails of people, have travelled the world with us ever since. Besides man, these two rodents are the most widespread and abundant mammals on earth.

And, though you might not like the description, it takes a pretty special animal to achieve the kind of dominance that these two characters have acquired. Both have extraordinary capabilities. For a start, they run and climb exceptionally well: a house mouse, for instance, can jump 30cm up to a ledge and survive a three-metre fall unhurt. Both species can also crawl into tight corners (a house mouse can squeeze through a 6mm gap) and walk tightropes, crossing the most precarious bridges. Rats, especially, are famous for their habit of embarking and disembarking from ships by taking short cuts across the ropes and rigging. Both rats and mice have followed people on hazardous journeys to the Antarctic continent and to countless isolated islands. Extremes of temperature do not deter them: rats have been known to live within fridges and chillers. They survive wind, rain and permanent snow.

Even now, in the midst of winter, both rats and mice may still be breeding – especially in the warm recesses of your home or under your floorboards. Little halts their production line, which is quite astonishingly efficient. Rats, for instance, are probably the most prolific mammals in the world in terms of productivity over a lifetime. A young female becomes sexually mature some 8–12 weeks after birth. Assuming that con-

Rats are remarkable creatures, though perhaps loved only by their mothers.

Gently does it: a house mouse dices with death.

ditions are good, she can mate and give birth as little as three weeks later, thus beginning her personal contribution to the rat population. The litter may contain up to nine young, which will then be sexually mature within a couple of months themselves. Meanwhile, a female can copulate again only 18 hours after giving birth, and can conceive again while still suckling her previous brood. All in all, theoretically, a rat could produce thirteen litters a year. The house mouse cannot quite match this rate, but can still produce 5–10 litters per year of up to eight young each. Either way, the end result is a lot of rodents.

None of this would happen were rats and mice not so astonishingly adaptable in what they eat. Any rodent would do well living in a grain store, as many do, but what sets the brown rat and the house mouse apart is that they can simply eat anything. House mice take a variety of plant material and insects in the wild state, but those that are our tenants will eat all our crumbs and more. They like cheese, of course, and also chocolate, but will also attempt to consume such oddities as tobacco, paste, glue and soap. Rats, meanwhile, are a little more predatory, taking such items as birds' eggs, frogs, carrion, various invertebrates and, believe it or not, the occasional mouse. Being excellent swimmers, there are even a few records of them catching and eating fish. These animals are in every sense omnivorous.

It would not, however, be correct to assume that rats and mice are indiscriminate in what they eat. In fact both rodents have a long history of being poisoned by people and can be surprisingly cautious of new foods. The brown rat, in particular, is described as strongly neophobic (a trait shared by some human children, although not, we hope, as a result of poisoning), often ignoring novel or familiar foods in unexpected places for months. For a rat, where one wrong bite is enough to cause premature death, suspicion is a survival strategy.

But for the rat to be fully opportunist, it must overcome this neophobia. And it seems that there must be some rats in any population always ready to take a risk – perhaps those overcome by hunger or curiosity. Once these individuals taste the new food, the rest of their clan smell it upon their breath and their natural resistance is quelled. Equally, however, if a rat passes a new source of food and then, shortly afterwards, meets a sick rat, it develops an aversion to this new food, whether or not it has tasted it. Furthermore, when a rat itself becomes sick, it seems to know instinctively what caused the problem, however many foodstuffs it might have sampled in between. The really extraordinary thing about this is that rats do eat some truly unusual things. Thus once upon a time a rat must have tasted glue or soap, survived, and communicated to the rest of its colleagues that this new food supply was fine.

Most of us, let's face it, don't like brown rats or house mice, and we have plenty of reason for this. Both rodents, after all, can cause damage to houses and contaminate food, and both can carry harmful pathogens and are a genuine health risk. But truly, most of them do very little harm, and they must surely qualify as among the most tenacious and remarkable of all our garden creatures.

The Sad Story of the Male Earwig

INSIDE OUR HOUSES the midwinter is, we hope, a time of Christmas cheer and conviviality. Outside in the garden, of course, such emotions are conspicuously lacking: robins still fight over territory, squirrels maintain their social hierarchies and foxes kill their prey, much as they do all year. But even so, the treatment of the male earwig at this time of year still raises an eyebrow. It is particularly uncharitable, even by the standards of our backyard jungle.

The sad thing is that it needn't have turned out this way. Just a month or two ago, when the ear-wigs were feeling amorous, two insects met up and decided to enhance their species' population. For an earwig, once the immediate necessities are over, this is actually quite an undertaking, involving building an elaborate nest in the soil. For many hours the two worked together to create a family cubby-hole, usually beneath a stone. They gnawed away at the earth with their mouthparts and brought piles regularly to the surface. After much effort, during which you would assume that male and female got to know each other well, they would finally have

Earwigs are among the best parents of all the garden's animals.

completed an impressive den with two chambers at the bottom. What could be better than such a safe house, with his quarters and hers placed close together in the bowels of the soil?

And yet, sadly, soon afterwards, the relationship must have disintegrated. As seems to happen so often, childcare responsibilities were to blame. Just when the female was about to lay the first of her 50 or so eggs, everything turned sour. The male, despite all his contributions, was violently evicted from the family home by the jaws and tail-forceps of the pregnant female. Cast out into the cold, dark soil, he succumbed to the season and died.

Now alone again and in charge of the eggs, the female earwig exhibits what is surely one of the most impressive stints of maternal care known in the insect world. She never leaves the eggs during the months that they are developing; they are not attached to her body, but she can move them around using her six legs. If danger threatens – and the soil is full of it – she will protect the eggs with her life, standing up to predators using her pincer-like rear end. Remarkably, since the burrow is sealed, the mother earwig cannot gather any food during the incubation period and thus fasts until the eggs hatch. She uses the stone at the top of the nest as an incubator, lugging all the eggs up against it if it heats up during the day and bringing them back down again if they start to overheat, each time checking that none gets left behind. If by any chance the eggs do become scattered, the mother will gather them up in her mouthparts – just like a cat or squirrel does, albeit with a much smaller brood.

Another of the earwig's routine duties is to lick each of the eggs at regular intervals. Although it has not yet been demonstrated exactly why she does this, circumstantial evidence points towards the application of fungicide, since eggs not treated like this tend to rot away.

With such devotion lavished upon them, it would be thoroughly unreasonable of any eggs not to hatch, and by the early spring the great moment approaches. Assiduous to the last, the mother lays them out singly upon the soil to prevent any crowding and watches, presumably breathless with anticipation, as the tiny nymphs begin to emerge. True to form, she quickly gathers them up and lies over them protectively.

You might now think that the female's vigil would be coming to an end, but there is still work to do. After all that effort, the mother is not yet ready to abandon her progeny. She continues to lick them periodically and defend them from enemies, and will even now make sorties outside to gather food, regurgitating it from her stomach into their waiting mouthparts.

Remarkably, it can be as late as June before the winter earwig clutch finally leaves the protection of the mother. By this time the nymphs will have moulted at least once, and usually twice, and will be a great deal larger than those tiny grubs that entered the world back in February or March. Even just hours before their departure, they still scurry back to mother if danger threatens.

After all the hard work, the great moment arrives: the nymphs hatch at last.

The tearful good-byes are not some temporary blip; these kids are not going to college only to return within weeks to have their washing done. This is a final gesture, and the female will henceforth have no power to recognise her progeny. Indeed any young that do not disperse might even end up at some later stage as food for their erstwhile protector.

Yet the overall impression is of the complete mother. And in this sense the female earwig exceeds many other, larger, garden species, including most birds and mammals, in its extraordinary parental dedication. What a shame for the male that he has no place in this caring family picture. One would surely expect him to play a useful part in protecting the nest, eggs and young, yet the female deems him surplus to requirements. The family courts invariably give lone custody to the mother, and the unfortunate, rejected father simply fades away.

The Christmas Bird

ON ALL THE Christmas cards you receive this year, which member of the wild garden community is likely to be better represented than any other? No prizes for guessing correctly. You might get the odd squirrel, fox or badger, and maybe a blue tit or a great tit if your friends know that you are a keen gardener, but the overwhelming favourite will undoubtedly be that popular garden icon, the robin. This bird has been depicted on Christmas cards since at least the 1860s, when it was used to represent the friendly postman, and in the present wildlife-friendly climate there is no sign whatever of the robin's yuletide popularity abating.

But what of this attractive character that adds such colour to December's dull, weary landscape? Is the robin worthy of its popularity? Does it really have any attributes that might communicate a festive message?

Well firstly, robins are undeniably appealing. This is not just because they have a pleasing orange-red splodge on the face and upper breast, but also because of their shape and demeanour. They have quite large, liquid eyes, which give them excellent vision in the deep shade of the forest, where 'wild' robins forage, and they thus look at humans with a mild, courteous expression. They also have an endearingly plump physique, exaggerated by their habit of frequently fluffing up their plumage. This is actually an energy-saving tactic, in which fluffing the feathers ensures that more insulating air is trapped between the air outside and the skin.

The tame framed: robins are surely the most confiding of all garden birds.

To add to their charming appearance, robins also have a habit of bobbing up and down, often while flicking their wings. This action is thought to enable them to judge distance effectively, much as we might stoop or crane our neck as we try to estimate how far away the local pub might be. They will do this when perching near people, which is simply being sensible in the face of a large and unpredictable creature, but comes across as an endearing curtsey.

Robins often have need of their curtseying, too, since they are undoubtedly the tamest of all our garden birds. It is robins that routinely come to investigate the gardener's progress, so often perching upon the temporarily stilled spade even while the handle is still warm. Countless gardeners have enjoyed their cup of tea as the robin works over the ground they have just tilled, fielding small invertebrates from under the nose of the delighted observer. The small birds will frequently take a few moments to sing upon a spade, showing extraordinary ease with their giant companions.

At first sight, such tameness is baffling. Why does the robin not wait until the gardener has finished before casting an eye over the work? It would seem, however, that the haste is a throwback to a technique evolved during the robin's past history as a forest bird. Robins have frequently been observed giving the gardener treatment to quite different animals of the forest, such as wild boar or deer, as they dig the soil or brush through foliage. They will even watch moles working close to the surface in order to pounce upon any fleeing worms. So it seems that the robin has always had a penchant for following the earth-moving work of others in order to snap up any tasty invertebrates that it reveals.

It is then merely a quick robin hop from watching gardeners to accepting their gifts. Robins come readily to bird-tables (though not usually to hanging feeders), and can also be trained to come to the hand, especially for mealworms. From the robin's point of view the benefits outweigh the risks of such actions, and they are soon unhesitant. Nevertheless, there are problems inherent in taming robins: much as these individuals delight people, they also fall prey more easily to the garden cat.

Another unusual characteristic of the robin is its indefatigable singing. This vociferous bird continues to defend its territory almost throughout the year, and its voice is especially dominant between September and early December. On a bleak December day it is thus not only the robin's appearance, but its song that enlivens the scene. You could even say that the sound brings cheerfulness when the season is at its lowest ebb.

If you really listen to it, though, the robin's song is not sensational. It never really grabs you, and if you wished to be unkind you could liken it to the forgettable piped musak that pollutes every shopping centre throughout the pre-Christmas period. The utterance is pleasant enough, and certainly very varied, but is far too weak ever to have the supercharged jolt of its close relative, the nightingale. You might think it surprising, therefore, that the robin is ever confused with that virtuoso singer of the late spring. But the confusion is easily explained: robins often sing at night.

It has been known for many years that robins can sing in the dark. One reason for this is that they have shade-adapted eyes, as mentioned above, which work at low light intensity, encouraging the birds to be active late into the winter evening. In urban and suburban areas, furthermore, some kind of light is always on throughout the night. Just recently a study also suggested that the darker hours favour transmission against a quieter human background, enabling the maximum benefit

to be gained by singing – broadcasting the message of territorial ownership loud and clear.

But whatever the reason for the night-time concert, it is undoubtedly a delightful sound. And to us it carries a further unintentional message. For bird song, essentially, is a spring activity. The Christmas period almost coincides with the Winter Solstice, that midwinter shift that determines the end of receding daylight, and sets off the long road to spring. So it is truly irresistible, on the night of Christmas Eve, to hear the delicate strains of this bird's voice in the darkness. At Christmas time the bird heralds the lengthening of the days: a time of cheer and hope. And what better reason – a brighter future – to have such a bird on your Christmas card?

A robin song in the depths of winter is a harbinger of the spring to come.

Epilogue

As the year comes to an end, the cycle of natural events in the garden certainly does not. The shortest day, towards the end of December, registers a click on the garden's dial, setting in motion the start of the next ascent to spring and summer. The cycle carries on inexorably.

Of course there will be some changes from one year to the next: more rain might fall; spring might be later, or summer hotter than usual. Events among the wildlife might alter, too: a mouse might move into your nest-box for the winter; blackbirds could have a great breeding season; there may be a 'plague' of wasps. These differences are part of the delight of gardens – and of life in general.

One thing doesn't change, though, and that is the garden's capacity to excite our sense of wonder. Every year, if you look carefully, you can spot something you've never seen before, be it a new species or some novel form of behaviour. This novelty will have nothing to do with you, but is an unsolicited gift from the natural world. And its sheer unexpectedness is one of the true sources of our wonder.

Many of us search hard for the remarkable, sometimes travelling to the far corners of the earth. Soon, though, the search begins to grate and the sense of novelty loses its lustre. But there is plenty of wonder closer at hand. It's there in your backyard. Just take a closer look.

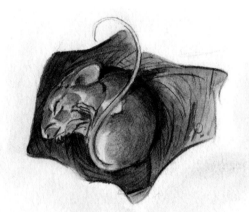

Acknowledgements

This book was a big departure for me as an erstwhile unreconstructed bird writer, so I owe my commissioning editor, Nigel Redman, a big thank you for believing in this project and taking a step of faith.

The task, as previously in the *Secret Lives* series, was made a good deal easier by Mike Unwin, to whom I owe a big debt of thanks for brilliant editing, great friendship and encouraging noises.

Peter Partington, in striving to depict living things without feathers, faced a similar challenge to mine. I need hardly say that he has risen to it triumphantly: the evidence is in these pages.

Once again, Paula McCann has handled the integration of text and illustration with expertise and aplomb. Many thanks also to Julie Bailey for being the long-suffering heartbeat of the project in production, and to Sophie Page for seeing it through to the end.

And thanks, as ever, to my family, who lived this book through some tough summer days when we would all like to have been outside. Thanks to Carolyn, my wife, for her loving support, and to our children Emily and Samuel. For the latter, I'm sorry I couldn't include the suggested elephants, but fairies managed to sneak in.

Bibliography

Attenborough, D. 2005. *Life in the Undergrowth.* BBC Books, London.

Bang, P. and Dahlstrom, P. 2001. *Animal Tracks and Signs.* Oxford Natural History. Oxford University Press, Oxford.

Beebee, T. 1985. *Frogs and Toads.* Whittet Books, London.

Beebee, T.J.C. and Griffiths, R.A. 2000. *Amphibians and Reptiles.* Collins New Naturalist. HarperCollins, London.

Brown, R, Lawrence, M and Pope, J. 1992. *Animals' Tracks, Trails and Signs.* Hamlyn Guide. Octopus, London.

Chinery, M. 1986. *Collins Guide to the Insects of Britain and Western Europe.* Collins, London.

Chinery, M. 1986. *Garden Creepy-crawlies.* Whittet Books, London.

Chinery, M. 1989. *Butterflies and Day-flying Moths of Britain and Europe.* Collins New Generation Guide. Collins, London.

Chinery, M. 1993. *Insects of Britain and Northern Europe.* 3rd edition. Collins Field Guide. HarperCollins, London.

Chinery, M. 1993. *Spiders.* Whittet Books, London.

Clark, M. 1994. *Badgers.* Whittet Books, London.

Conniff, R. 1996. *Spineless Wonders.* Souvenir Press, London.

Corbet, G and Southern, H. 1977. *The Handbook of British Mammals.* 2nd Edition. Blackwell Scientific Publications, Oxford.

Edwards, M. and Jenner, M. 2005. *Field Guide to the Bumblebees of Great Britain and Ireland.* Ocelli.

Gibbons, R. and E. 1988. *Creating a Wildlife Garden.* Hamlyn, London.

Golley, M. 2006. *The Complete Garden Wildlife Book.* New Holland, London.

Harris, S. and Baker, P. 2001. *Urban Foxes.* Whittet Books, London.

Harris, S. 2006. *Fox UK. BBC Wildlife* Magazine supplement. BBC Magazines, Bristol.

Holm, J. 1994. *Squirrels.* Whittet Books, London.

MacDonald, D. 1995. *European Mammals: Evolution and Behaviour.* HarperCollins, London.

MacDonald, D. 2006. *The Encyclopedia of Mammals.* Oxford University Press, Oxford.

Marshall, J.A. and Haes, E.C.M. 1988. *Grasshoppers and Allied Insects of Great Britain and Ireland.* Harley Books, Essex.

Morris, P. 2006. *The Hedgehog Book.* British Natural History Series. Whittet Books, London.

Neal, E. 1977. *Badgers.* Blandford Press, Poole, Dorset.

Perrins, C. 1987. *Birds of Britain and Europe.* Collins New Generation Guide. Collins, London.

Reader's Digest Association. 1984. *Field Guide to the Animals of Britain.* Reader's Digest, London.

Resh, V.H. and Carde, R.T. (eds). 2003. *Encyclopedia of Insects.* Elsevier Science, USA.

Richardson, P. 1985. *Bats.* Whittet Books, London.

Roberts, M.J. 1995. *Spiders of Northern Europe.* Collins Field Guide. HarperCollins, London.

Royal Horticultural Society. 2004. *RHS Good Plant Guide.* Dorling Kindersley, London.

Spedding, C. and Spedding, G. 2003. *The Natural History of a Garden.* Timber Press, Cambridge.

Waring, P. and Townsend, M. 2003. *Field Guide to the Moths of Great Britain and Ireland.* British Wildlife Publishing, Hampshire.

Young, M.R. 1997. *The Natural History of Moths.* T and A.D. Poyser, London.

Index